DATE DUE

OCT 4 00			

DEMCO 38-296

The Jossey-Bass Nonprofit Sector Series also includes:

Achieving Excellence in Fund Raising, *Henry A. Rosso and Associates*

The Board Member's Guide to Fund Raising, *Fisher Howe*

Boards That Make a Difference, *John Carver*

Conducting a Successful Capital Campaign, *Kent E. Dove*

The Corporate Contributions Handbook, *James P. Shannon, Editor*

Critical Issues in American Philanthropy, *Jon Van Til and Associates*

The Drucker Foundation Self-Assessment Tool for Nonprofit Organizations, *The Peter F. Drucker Foundation for Nonprofit Management*

Effective Fund Raising in Higher Education, *Margaret A. Duronio and Bruce A. Loessin*

Executive Leadership in Nonprofit Organizations, *Robert D. Herman and Richard D. Heimovics*

Governing, Leading, and Managing Nonprofit Organizations, *Dennis R. Young, Virginia A. Hodgkinson, Robert M. Hollister, and Associates*

Improving Corporate Donations, *Vic Murray*

The Jossey-Bass Handbook of Nonprofit Leadership and Management, *Robert D. Herman and Associates*

Leadership and Management of Volunteer Programs, *James C. Fisher and Kathleen M. Cole*

The Makings of a Philanthropic Fundraiser, *Ronald Alan Knott*

New Directions for Philanthropic Fundraising (quarterly)

Nonprofit Management and Leadership (quarterly)

Principles of Professional Fundraising, *Joseph R. Mixer*

Protecting Your Organization's Tax-Exempt Status, *Mark Bookman*

The Seven Faces of Philanthropy, *Russ Alan Prince and Karen Maru File*

Strategic Planning for Fund Raising, *Wesley E. Lindahl*

Strategic Planning for Public and Nonprofit Organizations, *John M. Bryson*

Taking Fund Raising Seriously, *Dwight F. Burlingame and Lamont J. Hulse, Editors*

Understanding Nonprofit Funding, *Kirsten A. Grønbjerg*

Women and Power in the Nonprofit Sector, *Teresa Odendahl and Michael O'Neill*

Reinventing Fundraising

Sondra C. Shaw
Martha A. Taylor

Reinventing Fundraising

Realizing the Potential
of Women's Philanthropy

Jossey-Bass Publishers • San Francisco

Copyright © 1995 by Jossey-Bass Inc., Publishers, 350 Sansome Street, San Francisco, California 94104. Copyright under International, Pan American, and Universal Copyright Conventions. All rights reserved. No part of this book may be reproduced in any form—except for brief quotation (not to exceed 1,000 words) in a review or professional work—without permission in writing from the publishers.

Substantial discounts on bulk quantities of Jossey-Bass books are available to corporations, professional associations, and other organizations. For details and discount information, contact the special sales department at Jossey-Bass Inc., Publishers. (415) 433–1740; Fax (800) 605–2665.

For sales outside the United States, please contact your local Paramount Publishing International Office.

TCF Manufactured in the United States of America on Lyons Falls Pathfinder Tradebook. This paper is acid-free and 100 percent totally chlorine-free.

Library of Congress Cataloging-in-Publication Data

Shaw, Sondra C., date.
 Reinventing fundraising: realizing the potential of women's philanthropy / Sondra C. Shaw, Martha A. Taylor.
 p. cm. — (Jossey-Bass nonprofit sector series)
 Includes bibliographical references (p.) and index.
 ISBN 0-7879-0050-8
 1. Fund raising—United States. 2. Women philanthropists—United States. I. Taylor, Martha A., date. II. Title. III. Series.
 HV41.9.U5S53 1995
 361.7'068'1—dc20   94-32448
                                                                          CIP

FIRST EDITION
HB Printing   10 9 8 7 6 5 4 3 2 1   Code 9507

The Jossey-Bass Nonprofit Sector Series

Contents

Preface

Women and giving. Not a radical thought, you might say. After all, women have always been givers, nurturers, and volunteers. What is different about this book is that we are talking about women giving not just their time but their money as well. We are talking about women going beyond the role of community volunteer and becoming philanthropists. And with their philanthropy, women will take their place among the people who shape society.

Like many other development professionals, we realized during the mid to late 1980s that we would need to look for new sources of money for our institutions. Public funds were not increasing at the same rate as our needs, and corporate and private dollars were not forthcoming rapidly enough to take up the slack. An examination of our donor rolls revealed that women were not giving to the same extent as men, and we wanted to know why.

We found, however, that many development officers at the time did not share our curiosity. They just accepted the fact that women give less to charity than men. Women simply do not make major gifts, they told us. A woman will give only if a man approves the gift or it is a bequest. And women do not designate their gifts responsibly to other than Band-Aid causes. Finally, women cannot and will not ask others for money. Face it, they said, women are not enlightened philanthropists.

Nonetheless, we wanted to know why. Could it be that development officers are not asking women to give? Are these officers taking the time to teach women how to give responsibly? Maybe women's motivations for giving are different from those of men. In that case, should development officers be looking at the way they ask women for gifts?

We shared our concerns with our colleagues at conferences and meetings across the United States, only to discover that we were not the only ones asking these questions. Women and a few men, both development officers and volunteer fundraisers, started calling us from all over the country. They expressed their interest, along with their thoughts, and in a few cases told us about programs that they had established to solicit more contributions from women for their institutions.

Women philanthropists began to get in touch with us as well. They told us that they were not being asked for money to the extent that they could respond and that when they did give, their gifts were often credited to their husbands; and they explained what went into their decisions to make major gifts to certain organizations and to avoid certain others.

It became clear to us that previous studies in philanthropy and fundraising spoke only to the ways in which men give and that women give for different reasons—reasons based on their experiences as women. We felt that through a better understanding of women's motivations our nation's institutions would benefit, not only from the enormous wealth that women control but also from the special values and insights that women can bring to the boardroom table. We also believed that to counter the stereotype of women as bad prospects for giving, we needed to detail the powerful impact women have had on philanthropy in the past, despite the lack of encouragement from society and the lack of recognition in textbooks. Women are continuing to wield this power today through their support of women's funds, women's colleges, women candidates, and human services. We have written this book to document the accomplishments and successes of women philanthropists and the organizations that have inspired them, as well as to show how other institutions and organizations can benefit from a new approach to fundraising.

The Study

In 1991 we began conducting interviews, focus groups, and discussions with more than 150 women philanthropists and scores of development professionals to discuss women and philanthropy. We asked them about their experiences with money and fundraising. We explored different approaches to fundraising, analyzing them from the viewpoints of donor, volunteer fundraiser, and development officer. In addition to personal interviews, we conducted focus groups and workshops across the country, and we continue to do so. Over the next year, we continued our interviews and began writing this book with three goals in mind:

- To identify the reasons why women have not been taken seriously as philanthropists, even though historically their contributions have significantly influenced our nation's human services, cultural, and educational institutions

- To document the growth of women's potential for giving, the experiences of women philanthropists, and model programs focusing on women's giving that have already been developed by certain nonprofit organizations and institutions

- To develop new conceptual program models for institutions and organizations to follow as they initiate programs tailored for their own female constituents

In the meantime, we participated in the creation of some new initiatives on the University of Wisconsin's Madison campus: the Women's Council of the Bascom Hill Society, the National Network on Women as Philanthropists, and the Center for Women and Philanthropy. In fall 1992 the center sponsored a two-day conference at the Wingspread Conference Center in Racine, Wisconsin, to establish a national agenda for women and philanthropy. This was the first time that women philanthropists, senior development officers, and corporate and foundation leaders had come together to discuss the role of women in philanthropy. The Wingspread discussions helped clarify the issues and provided us with the conceptual framework for this book. In addition, the conference showed us that understanding women's experiences, both as philanthropists and as development professionals, is critical to understanding women's giving.

The Book

This book is about leadership: the leadership of women philanthropists, both as givers and as volunteer fundraisers. It is also about the leadership of development professionals who are pioneering programs designed to reach out to women. Through the stories of these women and men, we see a new kind of fundraising emerging—one that we believe will ultimately define how all fundraising is conducted in this country: a dynamic and nonhierarchical strategy that connects people to the cause.

Much of the book describes educational institutions, their programs, and the women who give to them. This is because of our own personal background and because education, as is so often the case, is at the cutting edge of this movement. But we believe that these concepts can be applied to most organizations and have included examples demonstrating this.

Why has so much of the early work in the women's philanthropy movement taken place in the Midwest, particularly in Wisconsin? For one thing, Wisconsin has a strong tradition of educating women. Women have struggled here as elsewhere, but the door to the library was always open. In addition, many pioneers in the women's movement, including Carrie Chapman Catt, who fought for the vote early in the twentieth century, and many of the early leaders who worked for passage of the Equal Rights Amendment, came from the Midwest. This tradition continues with this latest frontier of the women's movement, philanthropy.

Another point deserves special notice. This book is primarily about American women philanthropists and development officers of European ethnicity. The philanthropic work of women of color has been examined in more detail by Emmett D. Carson, author of *The Hand Up: Black Self-Help in America* (1993). Moreover, the women's funds have set an excellent example of including women of all ethnic groups in their efforts to raise money for the improvement of the status of women in our society. We encourage more work in this area. In particular, a serious study of the philanthropy of women of color needs to be conducted by women of color; this will fill the blank pages in women's giving.

Audience

Reinventing Fundraising: Realizing the Potential of Women's Philanthropy is intended for readers interested in learning about philanthropy, philanthropic leadership, and the empowerment of women. It will be of particular interest to development officers, philanthropists, volunteer fundraisers, staffs and board members of nonprofit organizations, foundation and corporate executives, fundraising consultants, women's organizations, computer software firms, marketers, politicians and government officials, political fundraisers, educators, and anyone else interested in the status and roles of women in American society.

Overview of the Contents

This book begins with ten predictions about women and philanthropy that we believe will occur within the next five years. They provide the context for the chapters that follow.

Chapter One documents women's potential for giving and

women as funding prospects. It reviews the growing importance of women in the workforce and the nation's economy and describes their economic gains. The chapter also details the recent successes of women's fundraising for political candidates, women's colleges, and women's funds.

Chapter Two describes the contributions to society of several individual women philanthropists and shows the value of their work by tracing their contributions of time and funds to the nation's institutions and organizations.

Chapter Three profiles eight current female philanthropic leaders, from Portland, Oregon, to Miami, Florida. Each has a particular philanthropic interest: their support benefits ballet, women's funds, education, culture, and human services.

Chapter Four explores how and why women give and their characteristics as donors. These are revealed through comments from the women themselves and indicate the special motivations and strategies women bring to their giving. The psychology of women's giving has its origin in the social conditioning to which women are subjected from early girlhood on.

Chapter Five looks at common barriers to women's giving, including a sense of financial insecurity, an undeveloped sense of identity, unfamiliarity with financial matters, issues of money and power, questions of ownership and entitlement, a desire for anonymity, and common assumptions held by development officers and society regarding women as donors. The text gives suggestions for overcoming these barriers.

Chapter Six details a plan that organizations can apply to develop a gender-sensitive fundraising program. The text highlights the basics of conducting an internal assessment and proposals for beginning a program.

Chapter Seven examines how nonprofits can improve their communication with women. It provides specific suggestions, many of which are derived from successful corporate marketing campaigns. These include recognition of women's values, appreciation of their many social roles, and careful communication of the institution's image.

Chapter Eight outlines a complete multiyear program to attract more women as leaders and major donors. This ranges from establishing a task force to conducting focus groups and includes objectives and strategies in all operating plans and efforts.

Chapter Nine offers a program to train women volunteers to seek major gifts. It documents the formal training process used by the Women's Council of the Bascom Hill Society, University of Wisconsin, Madison.

Chapter Ten outlines the workings of a reinvented capital campaign that ensures women's representation in both the campaign leadership and the funds contributed. We use the best of the former capital campaign models and suggest ways to enhance campaigns to attract a new and diverse donor group.

Chapter Eleven describes four women's fundraising efforts that we have participated in: Very Special Arts Wisconsin; Sigma Kappa national sorority; the Women's Council of the Bascom Hill Society, University of Wisconsin, Madison; and A Fund for Women, in the Madison Community Foundation. Each project provided an opportunity to test new ideas and strategies. A case study of each of these efforts is provided, along with an analysis of what worked and what did not.

Chapter Twelve focuses on one woman philanthropist and fundraiser, Tracy Gary, and the organization she founded, Resourceful Women. Tracy is a pioneer in her efforts to work with women of wealth to help them understand their finances and invest their wealth wisely for their own benefit and that of society. A financial workshop that Tracy presented is described in detail.

Finally, in the Conclusion, we summarize our findings and those of other practitioners across the country to demonstrate the potential of women's giving to improve our world and the importance of knowing how to work with women prospects and donors.

Acknowledgments

In researching and writing this book, we became aware that our original motives had broadened. As we thought about how to increase women's giving, we saw the need for developing women's leadership, as well as their philanthropy. Our institutions need this, not only because they need money but also because they need women as a preeminent force for growth and change. As we learned about women's interests in children and human issues and put this together with the problems facing society today, we knew that we were on to something that could change the face of philanthropy forever.

We are deeply grateful to our two editors, Heather Shaw and Andrea Kaminski, without whom this book would never have been published. Our thanks go to Jean Manchester-Biddick and Kay Vaughan, who taught us the true meaning of philanthropy and birthed this idea with us; to Alma Baron, who taught us how to teach others; to Hamilton McCubbin, Mary Ann Shaw, and Anne Thompson, whose interest brought academic credibility to this movement; to Sylvia Ann Hewlett, who opened our eyes to children's and society's needs; to Judith E. Nichols, who believed in what we were doing and publicized our efforts right from the beginning; to Maddie Levitt, who shared our dream and whose support made all this possible; to Tracy Gary, whose example is an inspiration to so many of us; to our friends Brenda Hoyt, Jane Rasmussen, Carol Toussaint, and Judy Zerafa, whose encouragement kept us going; to our family members, Gary Antoniewicz, Nedra and Montelle Chase, Campbell Shaw, Christina Shaw, Laurie Shaw Smith, Esther Hougen Taylor, and Pamela Smith Taylor, who cheered us on and kept us focused; to the many women who shared their ideas and experience with us; to our many supportive male board members and colleagues, Robert M. Bolz, Donald Bowman, Bruce Flessner, Carleton Holstrom, Jack Ohle, Keith Pretty, Timothy Reilley, Robert Rennebohm, and James Vaughan; to our professors at our

Big Ten alma maters, who taught us to think, analyze, and reflect, which has enabled us to be part of this new frontier for the women's movement; and finally, to our grandmothers, mothers, aunts, and granddaughters, because we rejoice in the joy of families, where all philanthropy begins.

December 1994

Sondra C. Shaw
Kalamazoo, Michigan

Martha A. Taylor
Madison, Wisconsin

The Authors

Sondra C. Shaw is cofounder and codirector of the National Network on Women as Philanthropists. She is an author and speaker on women and philanthropy. She is assistant vice president for external affairs at Western Michigan University. The university is located in Kalamazoo and has a student population of twenty-seven thousand.

Shaw received her B.A. degree (1958) in education from Michigan State University and her J.D. degree (1985) from the Thomas M. Cooley Law School in Lansing, Michigan. She served six years as an elected official in Michigan and has more than eighteen years' professional experience, including her own public relations firm, sales and marketing, a legislative background, and fundraising consulting in Michigan, the District of Columbia, and Wisconsin. Her fundraising began in the political arena and included state representative and senate candidates and state and national party fundraising. She has raised money for both national and local nonprofit efforts.

Shaw has been a featured speaker on political and nonprofit fundraising at the state, regional, and national levels. She also serves on the steering committee for the Center for Women and Philanthropy at the University of Wisconsin, Madison, and chaired the

Wingspread Conference on Women and Philanthropy held in Racine, Wisconsin, in October 1992.

Martha A. Taylor is cofounder and codirector of the National Network on Women as Philanthropists, which is part of the School of Family Resources and Consumer Science, University of Wisconsin, Madison. She is vice president of the University of Wisconsin Foundation. Her primary work is with major gift fundraising. Taylor received her B.A. degree (1971) in history from the University of Wisconsin, Madison, and her M.S. degree (1975) in journalism from West Virginia University. Her master's thesis was titled "Educational Fundraising: Three Methods."

She is founder of the University of Wisconsin Foundation's Council on Women's Giving of the Bascom Hill Society, the first program at a large coeducational institution and eighth overall for the nation's institutions of higher education.

Taylor is nationally recognized as one of the leaders in the new women's philanthropy movement. Her studies on women as donors have been reported in the *New York Times Magazine* (Matthews, April 7, 1991). Her workshops and keynote talks, which she has presented in the U. S. and Europe, include "Women: The Forgotten Audience" and "Women and Philanthropy: Are Their Attitudes Different?" She has written several articles on women as philanthropists, including one with Sondra Shaw titled "Career Women: A Changing Environment for Philanthropy" (*National Society of Fund-Raising Executives Journal*, Fall 1991). She is a founding member of the Center for Women and Philanthropy in the School of Family Resources and Consumer Sciences, University of Wisconsin, Madison.

In fall 1991, Taylor and Shaw founded the National Network on Women as Philanthropists and launched its quarterly newsletter.

Taylor serves on the board of Lutheran Social Services of Wisconsin, the Wisconsin Auto and Truck Dealers Foundation, and

Arts Outreach of the University of Wisconsin, Madison. She is a past president of the Lutheran Campus Ministry of Wisconsin.

Ten Predictions for Women's Philanthropy

1. Women will take greater control of their own resources.

2. Women will make increasingly larger philanthropic gifts.

3. Most organizations and institutions will establish women's leadership and giving programs.

4. Nonprofit boards will become more balanced with respect to gender.

5. A new style of capital campaign will be developed to encourage sharing relationships and responsibility rather than competition.

6. Women's funds, women's political groups, and grassroots organizations will continue to gain women's support.

7. Women will leverage their gifts to ensure that their interests and values are matched with their philanthropic dollars.

8. Women will assume top philanthropic leadership positions as volunteer fundraisers and development officers.

9. As women move into decision-making positions within corporations, they will direct corporate giving toward programs addressing issues that reflect their values.

10. Women will insist that greater accountability be established and publicized by institutions and organizations.

Part One

Women: An Emerging Force in Philanthropy

Chapter One

Women as Important Prospects

Whether they inherit, earn, or marry money, women are becoming a powerful financial force, and they are increasingly looking at money as a way to change society for the better. As more women enter the professions, climb the executive ladder, and go into business for themselves, they are building fortunes and developing financial skills. Women are also in a position to come into significant amounts of money through inheritance. In the next twenty years, some $7 trillion will pass into the hands of baby boomers, and women outlive men by seven years (Tifft, 1992, p. 70). Yet women have not forsaken their commitment to a better world, and some have taken the lead in transforming philanthropy.

An example of the new woman philanthropist is Muriel Siebert, who was the first woman member of the New York Stock Exchange. She donates up to half the new securities commissions she underwrites to nonprofits chosen by her clients in the cities where she does business. In its two years of operation, the Siebert Entrepreneurial Philanthropic Plan (SEPP) has distributed more than $1.2 million to causes ranging from battered women to AIDS patients. This level of commitment to the public good, though unusual on Wall Street, has not hurt her business. In the meantime, her brokerage firm, Muriel Siebert and Company, has increased its business revenue by 20 percent every year since 1989.

Siebert has happily merged business acumen and financial success with a dedication to social change. She says, "I was raised to believe that when good things happen, you owe. And it's a good

3

feeling for me to realize that I am able to put together my brain, my heart and my knowledge of business to create something like this" (Greene, 1992, p. 7).

Another New York stockbroker, Patricia Winans, says she "got tired of stepping over homeless people," so she formed a foundation, From Wall Street to Your Street, to support programs that house the homeless and train the jobless. The foundation's assets represent more than half of Winans's commissions received on sales to clients who subscribe to the program. Although this reduces Winans's income, it has increased the firm's volume and tax deductions (Wynter, 1992).

Across the Atlantic, Anita Roddick is founder of the Body Shop, an international chain of natural cosmetics stores. With a net worth of $350 million in 1992, she was one of the five richest women in England. She has funded projects from Save the Whales to helping the homeless help themselves. In 1992 she opened a shop in Harlem, with 50 percent of the profits earmarked for community groups (Elmer-Dewitt, 1993; Brock, 1993).

A nasty proxy fight to gain control of her late father's company helped launch Karla Scherer's philanthropy. After winning the case in 1988, she sold the company but found that its assets were not being well managed. She gained control of her fortune and went on to question what she could do to ensure that society would not squander its assets. Her answer was to establish a $4 million foundation to help women who want to pursue business careers. She wanted to help women because, she said, "I think women are a squandered asset." Scherer herself serves as a female role model when she states, "Women skirt the issue of talking about money. You have to get used to the fact that money is power and you have to use it the way men do" ("Karla Scherer Channels Anger . . . ," Feb. 24, 1992).

Twelve years after first mixing up a new soft drink in her kitchen sink, Sophia Collier sold her Soho Natural Soda business, with annual sales of $25 million, to Seagram's. With the profits she was able to satisfy her dream of creating social change by joining other investors in buying the Working Assets Money Fund management firm, which invests only in firms with proven records of equal opportunity, environmental protection, fair labor relations, and sound financial management (Holley, 1992). Collier holds 60 percent of the firm's stock. "I represent more than 27,000 shareholders who want to invest their money in ways that effect positive social change. The thing is, what you say to the world, what you do with your money, what you eat and what you wear are all a part of an integrated whole" (Myers, 1993, p. 105).

Instead of joining a Fortune 500 company after graduating in the top 5 percent of Harvard Business School's class of 1985, Laura Scher became chief executive officer of a two-year-old consumer services company in San Francisco. The small company donates a portion of its profits to a pool that supports thirty-six nonprofit groups, and by 1992 it had given almost $1.5 million to such organizations as Amnesty International and the African Wildlife Foundation (Scher, 1992).

Philanthropist Helen Hunt used her inheritance to cofound the Dallas Women's Foundation and the New York Women's Fund. Her sister, Swanee Hunt, who founded the Denver Women's Foundation, personally contributed $250,000 to President Clinton's 1992 presidential campaign and raised another $1 million from other supporters. She says she did it because she believed Bill Clinton and Al Gore shared her concern about the homeless, the inner city, children, and mental health issues (Jones, 1992a).

Although few women have the financial resources of these leaders, many have the same deep commitment to the public good. And the number of women with wealth is rising. When fundraisers neglect this important group of potential major donors, they not only miss gift opportunities for their institutions but also sell women short. Development officers can play a vital role in educating women about how to manage their wealth and raising their sights as philanthropists working for a better world.

Women of Wealth

American women currently own 60 percent of the nation's wealth, and we have seen that some are using their financial resources to exert a powerful influence on society (Lederer, 1991). Although it is true that many older women still allow their money to be controlled by their husbands or male financial advisers, many others have taken control of their assets and are distributing them according to their own interests. Maddie Levitt of Des Moines, Iowa, is a good example of this self-empowerment. Following her divorce in 1987, Maddie began distributing money in her own name and for her own interests. She not only provided the initial leadership gift for the Campaign for Drake University but also chaired the successful $15 million campaign.

The assets owned by women are immense, and Internal Revenue Service figures indicate that of the 3.3 million Americans classified as top wealth holders in 1986, fully 41 percent were women, a figure substantially higher than only four years earlier. On average, the women in this privileged group were 6 percent wealthier than the men, held slightly more corporate stock, and were considerably less in debt. Though they had less insurance and personal property, the women owned more cash, real estate, and bonds (Matthews, 1991, p. 73). Women make up 35 percent of the country's fifty million stockholders (Belsky, 1992, p. 76). Clearly, their influence in financial affairs is of great importance and can be of much greater impact.

Much of the money described here is inherited money, which tends to be used quite differently by men and women. Men often invest their fortunes in business endeavors, while women are more likely to set up charitable funds and foundations that they administer themselves (Nichols, 1990a, p. 1). Twink Frey of Grand Rapids, Michigan, did just that when she established the Nokomis Foundation, which helped fund the Ms. Foundation's Women's Voices Project.

Younger women are also taking control of their money and currently represent half of the membership of the Funding Exchange, a philanthropic network of people who donate part of their inheritances to grassroots community groups. These young women, through their giving, assert that they are reconciling the power their money represents with their social ideals (Laurence, 1990, p. 14). Marjorie Fine, executive director of another alternative fund, the North Star Fund of Lower Manhattan, whose motto is "Change, not charity," describes the organization's typical donor as "a woman with a professional career in her 30s or 40s who received income from a family business, an inheritance, a legal settlement or some unexpected source" and as "older, 'mom' donors coming with their daughters" (Teltsch, 1992, pp. B1, B4).

Furthermore, women are more generous in making bequests than men. According to tax returns from 1986, in estates worth $5 million or more, 48 percent of female decedents made a charitable bequest, versus 35 percent of male decedents (Johnson and Rosenfeld, 1991, p. 30).

Career Women

The average income of working women is increasing at a far greater pace than that of men, according to the U.S. Census Bureau, and two-thirds of all jobs created in the 1990s are expected to be filled by women (Francese, 1992). Not only are women entering the workforce in enormous and unprecedented numbers not seen since World War II, but they are closing the wage gap and rapidly moving into positions of leadership. Though it is true that there are still few women chief executive officers of Fortune 500 companies, the number of women in middle management—from which the next generations of CEOs will be selected—now totals 44 percent and is growing. Other business areas where women are prominently employed are medicine and health management (66 percent), personnel and labor relations management (57 percent), accounting

(53 percent), and financial management (48 percent) ("Daughters Already at Work . . . ," 1993).

The traditional high-paying male-dominated professions of medicine, law, engineering, and accounting are benefiting from the rising numbers of women in their ranks, and in many law schools, female and male enrollment is now equal. And these women in the professions are supporting nonprofits: the 1992 political campaigns for women candidates were funded to a large degree by women, female attorneys in particular.

Advertising dollars and cause-related marketing will be strongly affected by the 33 percent of women in advertising, public relations, and marketing in agencies and corporations. Women are now moving into corporate positions in which they can influence decisions about how to distribute money supporting events and causes. They will have the opportunity to direct it toward areas women care about, such as breast cancer research, arts and culture, and the environment.

The tendency of women to drop in and out of the workforce as they raise their families has in the past deterred the upward movement of women's wages and positions of power within an organization. However, today's need for two-income families and the desire for self-sufficiency in uncertain times has a led more women to plan for a lifetime of work. In addition, many women are delaying marriage, postponing childbirth, or remaining single ("Life After Nannygate," 1993, p. 49). Though it may seem that these factors would inhibit charitable giving, recent findings indicate that women are more likely to give than men (Tiehen and Andreoni, 1993, p. 40).

Women Entrepreneurs

Women-owned businesses have increased from 2.6 million in 1982 to 6.5 million in 1992 and now employ more people than the Fortune 500 companies (Nasar, 1992). Business ownership is strongly tied to educational attainment, and because women are receiving more college degrees than men, the numbers of women business owners are expected to continue growing over the next decade, reaching 50 percent by the year 2000 (Bamford, 1993, p. 49).

With $16 billion in sales and revenues from the 50 top women-owned companies in the U.S. in 1994 (employing more than 175,000 people), it is easy to understand the amount of influence that this group of women will wield in America in the next century ("NFWBO and *Working Woman* . . . ," 1994, p. 4). Areas in which this influence will be felt most are business management style and corporate decisions about philanthropy.

These female entrepreneurs are a much different group from their male counterparts, with separate motivations and goals. Men's business motivations, according to Joline Godfrey (1993), are centered around getting rich quickly, fast growth, and a lifelong devotion to their jobs. Women, however, often begin a business because of frustration with the "glass ceiling," because they need more flexibility in their work schedules, or even because they want to create change (O'Hare, 1992).

Recognizing the good business value of corporate philanthropy, these new women entrepreneurs are proving to be generous to non-profits as their businesses grow. Pleasant Rowland, president and chief executive officer of the Pleasant Company, a Wisconsin doll manufacturer with annual sales of $108 million in 1993, is one of the new breed of female entrepreneurs. Established in 1986, Rowland's company already provides $350,000 a year to children's causes, including the Madison Children's Museum.

Women's Giving Patterns

Women vary in how much they give and how they make their gifts, depending on their age and life stage, ethnicity and religious background, and values and philanthropic interests. Following is a breakdown of giving patterns by various groups of women.

New Older Women

Born between 1928 and 1945, these women were affected by the Great Depression (either directly or through their parents), World War II, the advent of television, and, perhaps most important, the women's movement. They grew up without role models during the secure but conformist 1950s and had to invent themselves.

These are the women who are presently in their fifties and sixties and potentially in a position to be major donors. Many are high achievers but may have come to a profession late in life. The new older women are the first generation to give significant amounts of money that they themselves have earned. For the first time, large numbers of women are collecting their own pensions.

They represent the first generation of women appointed to fill positions on boards heretofore open only to men. They were raised in a *Father Knows Best* world, and many have achieved their success by reading men wisely and winning their trust. These women gained positions of authority because they were smart, acceptable, and seemingly nonthreatening, but most are also aware of having been in the right place at the right time.

This background makes them good prospects for funding programs designed to help women succeed in careers and positions of leadership. Also, because the new older women are spending nearly as much time taking care of their elderly parents as they did raising children, they are excellent candidates for funding programs for the elderly. Education played a major role in their lives, often involving a degree attained after child rearing, and they are frequently on the forefront of environmental movements. Hence these new older women are prospects with important connections to a diverse array of nonprofit causes.

The struggle they overcame to achieve their goals has given many new older women a degree of self-confidence and assurance that can be intimidating. However, their successes have also given them the confidence to follow their beliefs, and they are strong supporters of education, children, the environment, and women.

Baby Boomers

According to demographer Harold Hodgkinson, 74 million baby boomers, the best-educated generation of all time, will be writing "an enormous number of wills in the next decade—and they have an extraordinarily small number of children. That translates into a lot of dollars to philanthropy" (Shaw and Taylor, 1991, p. 48).

This generation, which came of age during the Vietnam War era, is acutely aware of society's problems. In light of the fortunes that they are projected to own in the future and their social conscience, boomers (born between 1945 and 1965) are poised to be most generous to nonprofits. A Roper Organization poll reported that they have already demonstrated their generosity, with 65 percent giving money to charities in 1989, compared to 63 percent of people aged forty-five to fifty-nine and 59 percent over age sixty-five (Millar, 1990, p. 1). Furthermore, baby boom women are increasingly more willing to give. In 1991 some 2.5 percent of their household incomes went to charity, up from 1.8 percent in 1989. This signifies an increase in the average contribution from $769 to $1,089 in two years (Richman, 1992, pp. 1, 11).

Baby boom women have a crucial financial advantage over the preceding generation of women: education. They are much more likely to have gone to college, and their education and experience in the workforce will translate into higher salaries (Waldrop, 1991, p. 27).

Where do boomers give? They are most likely to give locally, where they can see the results of their charity. Baby boom women, according to direct-mail expert Roger Craver, are "the group most willing to put their money on the line to get the social changes they want" or to fight the changes they do not want (Apple, 1992, p. 1).

Young Women

It has been suggested that young women (born after 1950) will form the financial core of social action advocacy movements during the 1990s by supporting causes such as environmental protection, abortion rights, and gun control. Almost half of the total socially conscious donor community earns more than $50,000 a year, three-fifths are professionals or executives, and 60 percent are women (Goss, 1991, p. 21).

Certainly, young women's values reflect concerns for making the world a better place. A 1991 poll of 210,000 students enrolled at 421 colleges and universities, conducted by the Higher Education Research Institute at the University of California, Los Angeles, indicates that influencing social values, helping others who are in difficulty, participating in a community action program, and promoting racial understanding are concerns of greater importance to female than male students (Collison, 1992, p. A35). Although not much research is currently available about this age group, more will be known as its members become a force in the corporate and philanthropic worlds during the next decade. Already, the Center for Women and Philanthropy at the University of Wisconsin, Madison, Syracuse University, and others are collaborating on research projects to track these young women as donors.

Ethnically Diverse Women

We are a nation of diversity. By the year 2050, white people of European descent will represent only 53 percent of the population of the United States ("U.S. Ethnic Diversity to Grow," 1992, p. A3). To ignore this projection would be folly for fundraisers, yet very little information exists about minority giving. The polls conducted up to this point, however, suggest that philanthropy in ethnic communities is primarily unstructured and occurs among families: for example, sending money to relatives in native countries to meet emergency needs or sharing with friends and those in need in the community, church, or fraternal organizations. However, an Independent Sector/Gallup survey reveals that black and Hispanic Americans are not asked by nonprofits to give at the same rate as other groups but that when asked, they are more likely to contribute (Hodgkinson and Weitzman, 1992). The logical conclusion is that nonprofits are overlooking minorities as prospects (much as they overlook women) and are thereby missing important fundraising opportunities.

Nonprofits will benefit from a better understanding of multicultural giving. One way to accomplish this is to include women of all ethnic backgrounds on our nonprofit boards and staffs. A more detailed discussion of the philanthropy of women of diverse ethnic groups follows.

African-American Women

African-American women are making significant gains in economic status, due in large measure to a 300 percent increase in college enrollment from 1965 to 1985. While they are increasing their numbers in technical, sales, and administrative occupations, they are also closing the wage gap between themselves and white women (Nichols, 1990a, p. 95). In addition to getting more education, African-American women are benefiting from the recognition by employers of the benefits of diversity in the workplace. In fact, college-educated black women work in almost the same proportion and the same professions as their white female counterparts ("Working Women . . . ," 1991, p. 82). Thus just as white career women are good prospects for fundraisers, so are black career women. Moreover, affluent blacks give as much to charity as whites, according to Emmett D. Carson, economist and program officer in governance and public policy at the Ford Foundation and author of *The Hand Up: Black Philanthropy and Self-Help in America* (1993). Research also indicates that black women are very charitable, no matter what

their income level; however, they tend to have little trust in organized charities and give primarily to their churches (Carson, 1987).
It has been suggested that black women grow up observing the
importance of community churches and are expected to continue
the tradition of support.

Black women philanthropists and celebrities currently advocate
education (Camille Cosby, Oprah Winfrey, Whitney Houston),
AIDS research and education (Dionne Warwick, Gladys Knight),
abused and neglected children (Melba Moore), and community
social problems (Marla Gibbs) ("Blacks Who Give . . . ," 1990,
pp. 64, 66, 68–69). Career women, such as stockbroker Patricia
Winans, mentioned earlier in this chapter, and capitalist JoAnn
Price, who is raising venture capital to help minority-owned businesses, represent the younger black career women who want to help
others and give back to their communities (Richards, 1992).

Hispanic Women

Demographers point out that Hispanics constitute the fastest-
growing ethnic population in the United States. The income level
of Hispanic women is rising as they are receiving more education,
entering the workforce in increasing numbers, and acquiring positions as managers and professionals (Nichols, 1990a, p. 52). Furthermore, this is the only ethnic population in which the women
are more charitable than the men (Hodgkinson and Weitzman,
1992). Their philanthropic interests include higher education, religion, family, and the community.

Hispanics in Philanthropy, a national affinity group, posits as its
goals the promotion of philanthropy education and the support of
Latino communities in the United States. Members work in
national foundations, and they have regional committees in Boston,
New York, Chicago, Miami, El Paso, San Francisco, and Los Angeles. The following statement, which appeared on the cover of their
1991 annual report, reveals that this community's concerns mirror

those of many women: "Too often, if you look at the world through Hispanic eyes, you see war, or violence, or racial strife. Whether in our cities in America or in our other countries of origin, we need to work together to create a vision of peace."

Jewish Women

Jewish women control more wealth than ever before, according to Susan Weidman Schneider. She points out that Jewish women's money comes as a result of their being "wage earners, beneficiaries of estates, directors of companies, board members of foundations and women's funds, and the ones in charge of running family foundations." This situation is likely to continue, as American Jewish women are the best-educated group of women in the country, with 64 percent between the ages of twenty-five and forty-five holding college degrees. This figure compares with 18 percent of other white women (Schneider, 1993, pp. 6, 8).

The culture of giving is strong in the Jewish community, as evidenced by the $2 million raised annually by the women's division of the Milwaukee Jewish Federation and the $7 million by the women's division of the Miami Jewish Federation. In Milwaukee, the women's division has been raising about one-quarter of the federation's total contributions, and that proportion is rising, according to development director Evelyn Garfinkel.

Women working with the United Jewish Appeal solicit funds through "caucuses," group fundraising sessions that feature very personal accounts by the participants of how they have lived their lives and why they consider it important to give to Jewish programs. Garfinkel explains that Jewish women are trained and expected to solicit money. She and Schneider both report that when Jewish women give to Jewish organizations, they often want to see their money applied to women's issues.

In Milwaukee, women receive training and campaign books from the national office. The solicitation is very structured. Contrary to the male model in Jewish federations, in which fundraising sessions are held in a large hall in a hotel, the Milwaukee women solicit gifts at gatherings in people's homes. Prospects receive an invitation to the session, with a stated gift amount for them to consider. Upon arrival at the home, they spend some time socializing and are then escorted into rooms, where their gift is privately solicited by two women.

Asian-American Women

According to *Marketing to Women*, Asian women are the fastest-growing and most affluent minority women, though it should be noted that the Asian cultures are very diverse with respect to the amount of control women have over money. In 1989 Asian-American women made up 2.7 percent of the nation's female citizens, with 67 percent of them working for pay. Most Asian-Americans live in the metropolitan areas of the western states and have high levels of education ("Minorities: Asian," 1990; "Asian Americans," 1991, p. 59). Though we know little about the philanthropic interests of this segment of the population, we can learn something about their attitudes by noting their confidence in their current economic situation and their optimism about the future ("Minorities/Shopping . . . ," 1992). With high levels of education, good jobs, later marriages and childbearing, less marital disorder, and enthusiastic expectations, Asian-American women appear to be excellent fundraising prospects for colleges and universities.

Support for Women's Colleges

If little is yet known about who the major women philanthropists are, even less is known about their motivations and how they have applied their philanthropy. Records at most nonprofits do not reveal much information about women because they have been set up to provide information about men. A traditional cause that women have supported with their philanthropic dollars, however, is education, and the unprecedented success of fundraising campaigns by women's institutions in recent years attests to women's increasing charity clout.

The development staffs of women's colleges have been educating themselves for years about their graduates and how to approach them for money. Their success has been phenomenal: in 1992 fully 40 percent of the twenty institutions and universities rated highest in terms of alumni support per student were women's colleges (McDonell, 1992, p. 23). This is even more astounding when one realizes that these institutions account for only 20 percent of all colleges and universities in the United States (Hall, 1992, p. 23).

These women's colleges have discovered how best to approach their graduates. In the 1993 academic year, the average women's gift to a seven sister's college was $947, while the average gift to a similar historically men's college was $798 (Morgan, 1994). This increased giving at single-sex institutions can be attributed to higher earnings, greater financial sophistication, more discretion over disposition of family income, and more effective solicitation (Menschel, 1992, p. 6).

Nicki Tanner, cochair of the highly successful Wellesley College campaign, says, "The first three liberal arts colleges to raise more than $100 million were women's colleges (Smith, Wellesley and Mt. Holyoke), and two women's colleges (Wellesley and Smith) during the last two years ranked number one and number two in total support among all liberal arts colleges—that is, they raised the most dollars, had the highest percentage of giving and received the largest gifts." She goes on to say, "It makes sense for fund raisers to look seriously at women's potential for philanthropic giving. After all, women make up half the population . . . and pay their debts early" (Tanner, 1992, p. 4).

Why do women give more to women's colleges than to coeducational schools? One obvious reason is that single-sex institutions provide women with leadership positions. Another is that these women are trained at an early age that they are expected to support their alma mater.

Women and Political Support

Women represent 52 percent of the population. In 1990 a total of 60.2 million women were registered voters, versus 53 million men. Thus women have considerable political power just in terms of their numbers. Recently, however, women have begun to realize that their clout goes beyond their own vote. They know that their dollars help, too.

Political parties and candidates are beginning to pay attention to this enormous market, which is challenging the old approaches to political fundraising. In particular, 1992 was a record-breaking year for female support of women political candidates. This unprecedented aid resulted in female candidates' receiving only $10 million less than males for House and Senate races. One need only look at Senator Barbara Boxer from California, who raised over $10 million for her election, more than any other senatorial candidate. Two-thirds of her money came from women, who until then had never been taken seriously as donors by the national parties or the candidates themselves.

One of the most important events during the 1992 elections was October's Million Dollar Day, which brought Hillary Clinton and Tipper Gore to Denver for a daylong issues forum. Denver philanthropists Swanee Hunt and Merle Chambers invited well-to-do women from all over the country to attend the event. Although these women were prosperous, giving top dollars was often a stretch, as many had not previously been involved in politics or independent philanthropy. The women had been moved to become involved, however, by Anita Hill's testimony at Clarence Thomas's Supreme Court nomination hearings, rhetoric at the Republican convention, and government lassitude regarding social issues.

The event was not of the sort that women have traditionally been associated with, such as charity balls and auctions. Rather, a diverse group of women was encouraged to attend. Some who were not wealthy but were informed and interested in the issues also sought to attend, and these women were "sponsored" by others who gave enough money for themselves and a guest.

Even the theme was different—and serious: "Serious women, serious issues, serious money." Whereas in the past, women have been responsible for many of the activities that go on during elections, such as staffing phone banks, distributing literature, and stuffing envelopes, this time they were being asked to give big money, regardless of whether asking or being asked made them uncomfortable. They also understood that money can buy a level of authority and the power to change things and be reckoned with. Not only had $1 million never been raised from 150 women in a single day before, but it had never even been attempted (Apple, 1992; Jones, 1992b).

Buttressed by these and other successes, women's groups such as Emily's List (Early Money Is Like Yeast—It Rises), WISH (Women in the Senate and House), the Fund for a Feminist Majority, the National Organization for Women (NOW), the Women's Campaign Fund, and the National Women's Political Caucus also raised unprecedented sums for female political candidates in 1992. With the astonishing amounts of money raised by these groups (Emily's List raised $6 million, more than four times what it raised in 1990), many political professionals had to acknowledge the impact women have on the political process (Abramson, 1992).

As it turns out, many of the new female political contributors are baby boomers under forty-five years old who are willing to put their money on the line for the social changes they envision. These baby boomers took seriously the task of addressing the social agenda, whose issues they saw as the environment, health care, human needs, the homeless, equality, and the so-called women's issues, including child care and family leave (Center for the American

Woman and Politics, 1992). As a group, women gave more money to Democrats, whom they perceived as better able to deal with these issues. On election day, 7 percent more women than men voted for the winning Democratic ticket.

Growth of Women's Funds

Women's funds are providing a hearty accompaniment to the activity in other areas of women's giving. There are more than sixty women's funds in the United States and Canada, and most are less than ten years old. Not only are the funds enjoying a period of extraordinary growth in total numbers, but they are also raising money. According to the National Network of Women's Funds, annual donations rose from $12.6 million in 1991 to $15.4 million in 1992, an increase of 22 percent (Millar, 1993, p. 16). Since 1985, women's funds have raised almost $81 million and have given away $36.2 million in grants to programs serving women and girls. The number of women's funds has grown from thirty-four in 1985 to sixty-three in 1992—an 85 percent increase in just seven years.

The rapid growth of women's funds is due largely to the recognition of the feminization of poverty. In their efforts to address this problem, women began to take note of how little money from large foundations and corporations is directed toward women's and children's programs (less than 5 percent). They also uncovered another discrepancy: the dearth of women on foundation boards. This helped explain why so little money was going to support women, despite the fact that women and children represent three-quarters of the nation's poor. While some women began to advocate for more funds from the traditional organizations, others established new sources of revenue. This provided a welcome outlet for many wealthy women who had not previously found the right cause or reason to give.

Carol Mollner, executive director of the National Network of

Women's Funds, in a presentation to the Fund for Women in Madison, Wisconsin, said the following:

> The truth is, women and children make up 75 percent of [Americans living] in poverty; single-parent households headed by women are the fastest-growing segment of our homeless population. We all know about violence against women, and we understand the many other challenges women face. We have found that our donors have both the vision and a passion for justice. They are using their resources boldly and are bringing the power of their money to bear on that vision. We are also democratizing and diversifying philanthropy so that it truly represents all segments of the community. Every woman is asked to be a donor at whatever level she can afford. Being donors makes us "stakeholders" who will work to ensure that the fund is responsive to all communities. Women's funds aren't set up in the hierarchical model of some people as donors, others as "recipients."

Gifts to women's funds range from a hundred women giving a thousand dollars each in Madison, Wisconsin . . . to women in a battered women's shelter in central Minnesota giving $58 . . . to gifts of a million dollars or more.

Mollner stresses that women should not divert any money that they are currently giving to other women's organizations—these should be new dollars. "Our goal is to increase resources for women and girls," she says.

Women's fund grants support the following activities:

- Safety projects such as battered women's shelters, rape crisis programs, and support for women leaving prostitution

- Arts and cultural programs for women artists and writers

- Economic programs benefiting women and girls

- Women's health and reproductive rights
- Civil rights and social justice
- Leadership and empowerment, particularly for girls and young women
- Scholarships
- General advocacy and services

Women's funds are very creative in their fundraising methods, which include special events, such as luncheons and dinners with featured speakers and commemorative books honoring women who have made a difference. Still, the approach most commonly used is a personal, one-on-one request.

The time for increased giving by women is clearly here. With women rapidly moving into positions of political and economic power, they are in command of tremendous amounts of money, more so than in previous generations, whose women owned but did not always control their wealth. Today's younger women will be redefining the ways in which people give because they are doing so in new ways and for reasons quite distinct from those of men. Their wealth and their concern about the future will influence dramatically the strategies employed by the organizations and institutions competing for money. We who do the asking will have to develop new approaches that will appeal not only to white women but also to minority constituencies. The potential is enormous, and so are the challenges.

Chapter Two

The History of Women's Philanthropy

Although fundraisers have only recently identified women's philanthropy as an important topic, individual women have long been leaders in their charitable contributions and work. The late nineteenth and early twentieth centuries, in particular, saw women expressing their vision for a better society through their philanthropy. These pioneering women used their money to establish institutions and improve conditions for the poor and ill. This gave them an opportunity to be creative and make a difference despite the social restrictions that did not allow them to work for a salary.

Women's contributions to philanthropy have been a gradual and often reluctant revelation to modern historians. Only in the past decade have scholars come to accept that women's absence from the pages of our history books does not mean that their participation was unremarkable. Rather, editors and writers did not consider the role of women important enough to document, and many of the women themselves, in their desire for anonymity, too frequently kept their magnanimity secret.

Since our schoolbooks have generally not told us of women's contributions, we must ask ourselves, Who were these invisible mothers and wives who, individually and collectively, set about to establish schools, hospitals, churches, libraries, symphony orchestras, museums, and gardens? The following brief biographical sketches describe the lives and work of a representative sampling of women, their organizations, and their activities. They are separate threads of a tapestry that, like most tapestries, was created by women whose names have gone largely unrecorded. The sketches reveal that since as far back as the 1700s, women have affected every part of society, from education to environmental preservation. Their vision, volunteerism, and philanthropy contributed much to society and the growth of this nation.

For example, Anna Richardson Harkness distributed $40 million dollars of her own money during her lifetime in the nineteenth century. Her philanthropy spanned the areas of education, health, science, and the arts. She gave $6 million to Yale University and a twenty-two-acre site valued at $4 million to Columbia University for a medical school and hospital. She founded and endowed with $20 million the Commonwealth Fund, one of the first American foundations to be established by a woman. She also gave generous annual gifts to the New York Public Library, the Museum of Natural History, and the Metropolitan Museum of Art.

In 1888 her husband died, leaving her an inheritance of $50 million, which she managed for the next thirty-eight years, increasing the value of the original estate to $85 million. At her death in 1926, Harkness designated most of her fortune to nonprofit organizations, including an additional $22 million to the Commonwealth Fund (McHenry, 1980a, pp. 176–177).

Social Responsibility

Although the early philanthropic work of American churches focused on missionary efforts abroad, many of the women supporting these efforts became concerned with problems closer to home. Their initial endeavors were directed at less fortunate women and children—a natural and socially justifiable step from the care and management of a private home. This church-inspired form of labor-intensive philanthropy was considered by both men and women a kind of domestic obligation to society.

Out of the women's organizations within the churches rose the nation's first independent charitable organizations, including the

Female Society for the Relief and Employment of the Poor, established in Philadelphia in 1793, and the Society for the Relief of Poor Widows with Small Children in New York City.

Isabella Martha Graham: Society for the Relief of Poor Widows with Small Children

Despite her formidable inheritance, Isabella Martha Graham, a widow, was aware of the often overwhelming difficulties of raising a family and providing for it at the same time. In 1797 she joined fifteen other women to organize the Society for the Relief of Poor Widows with Small Children in New York City. Through employment services, education, and the efforts of scores of female volunteers, the Widows' Society aided ninety-eight women and more than two hundred small children during its first winter. By 1816 it was supporting two hundred women with five hundred children (Lerner, 1992, p. 191). The society was very popular, and by the turn of the twentieth century, nearly every town of any size had a similar organization of its own, organized and managed by affluent women.

Margaret Gaffney Haughery: New Orleans Female Orphan Asylum

The entrepreneurial spirit was surely a dominant trait in this feisty and extremely successful nineteenth-century woman. An uneducated immigrant from Ireland, Margaret Gaffney Haughery used her considerable talents and hard work to save up to buy two cows, which eventually became a herd that supplied a dairy that she established. She also began the first steam-operated bakery in the South, and as many women business owners of today are doing, she quietly gave away much of her profit to address society's needs. Some of the groups that prospered from Haughery's financial success were the New Orleans Female Orphan Asylum, Saint Vincent's

Infant Asylum, and "free markets" for soldiers' families during the Civil War. At her death in 1882, despite her generosity, her estate was worth half a million dollars, the majority of which she left to religious and charitable institutions (McHenry, 1980a, p. 181).

Rebecca Gratz: Female Hebrew Benevolent Society

Rebecca Gratz was a celebrated beauty in Philadelphia society in the first half of the nineteenth century. She was also the model for the character Rebecca in Sir Walter Scott's epic novel *Ivanhoe*. Her first philanthropic involvement was with the Female Association for the Relief of Women and Children in Reduced Circumstances, in Philadelphia. Later she became interested in improving the religious education of Jewish children. In 1838 she established the Hebrew Sunday School Society of Philadelphia, under the auspices of the Female Hebrew Benevolent Society. Gratz's society served as the model for several others (McHenry, 1980a, p. 165).

Philanthropy of African-American Women

Just as children were the focus of concern for many female philanthropists, so were women themselves, particularly older women. The Phillis Wheatley Home Association, serving elderly African-American women, was organized in Detroit, Michigan, in 1897 by twenty-four black women. The group ultimately purchased property and furnished a building for twelve elderly women (Lerner, 1992, pp. 197–198). The Phillis Wheatley Home Association also established houses in safe areas of larger cities for single young African-American women and girls (Davis, 1982, p. 90).

Efforts like these were the initiative of black women's clubs, scores of which were organized in the late nineteenth century for the purposes of social welfare and charity. A larger organization, the National Association of Colored Women, whose motto was "Lifting As We Climb," focused on helping the homeless, supporting an employment service, and providing day-care centers and kinder-gartens (Meier, 1963, p. 135). The philanthropy of these women was born of a belief in mutual aid. Their endeavors grew out of the mutual aid societies and cooperative medical programs formed ear-lier in the nineteenth century to oppose slavery, combat lynching, and assist freed slaves (McDonell, 1992). By the early twentieth century, the smaller clubs were actively organizing programs and donating their time and money all over the United States to pro-vide health care and health education, help destitute community members, improve education, and teach girls about sexual respon-sibility (McDonell, 1993, p. 3).

Volunteer Fundraising

Just as the church provided women with a legitimate environment for their philanthropy, the Civil War gave them clear and unprece-dented opportunities to volunteer time and money in the name of the war effort. It was also the war that granted women their premier occasion at major fundraising.

Jane Currie Blaikie Hoge: Evanston College for Ladies

When the Civil War broke out, Jane Currie Blaikie Hoge, like many others of her class, was working in homes for orphans and the poor in Philadelphia and Chicago. But when her two sons enlisted to fight on the side of the Union, she began volunteer nursing at a nearby Chicago army base. There she met Dorothea Dix, superin-tendent of army nurses, and began to recruit nurses for the western region.

Hoge took advantage of the period's relaxed social restraints and seized the opportunity to manage her own financial affairs. This led to the eventual direction of more than a thousand aid societies and several soldiers' homes with her friend Mary A. Livermore. Hoge and Livermore also raised $70,000 in four months for the relief effort from one special event, a precedent repeated in several other large cities the following year.

After the war, Hoge's interest in the education of young women prompted a fundraising campaign to begin the Evanston College for Ladies, which opened in 1871. The college was later consolidated with Northwestern University (McHenry, 1980a, p. 193).

Jane Addams: Hull House

Jane Addams was awarded a Nobel Peace Prize in 1931 after pouring her money, time, and energy into providing educational, vocational, and domestic training and playground and nursery care for women and immigrants. Addams's supporters were frequently recent graduates of the newly founded women's colleges. She felt that these young women benefited from the experience, especially the contact with the less fortunate (McHenry, 1980a, pp. 3–4). Her drive and dedication often inspired other upper- and middle-class women to contribute their fortunes as well.

Although Addams's name is the one most often cited in connection with early social welfare philanthropy, there were countless others involved.

- Anne Parrish, a Philadelphia Quaker, founded the Aimwell School for needy girls as well as the first charitable organization for women in America, the House of Industry, which provided employment.

- Josephine Marshall Jewell Dodge sponsored the Virginia Day Nursery in New York City, to care for working women's children, and the Jewell Day Nursery, a daycare and nursery school for immigrant children.

- Sarah Platt Hines Doremus established, between 1850 and 1866, the Woman's Hospital, the Woman's Union Missionary Society, the Presbyterian Home for Aged Women, and the New York House and School of Industry.

- Dorothy Leib Harrison Wood Eustis lent her fortune and her intelligence to the development of the Seeing Eye dog and related training schools.

- The family values of sisters Caroline Phelps and Olivia Phelps Stokes directed their philanthropy to a number of social causes, including the establishment of the Phelps-Stokes Fund to support improved tenement housing in New York and the education of students from India and Africa, as well as both black and white Americans (McHenry, 1980b).

Cultural Institutions

Contrary to Europe, where men controlled the arts through their financial, educational, and religious organizations, in the United States women have been regarded as the "keepers of culture." While husbands and fathers were occupied with free enterprise and the pursuit of a legacy, American women traditionally turned a great deal of their attention and initiative to the arts. They not only collected and conserved existing art but also promoted new artists and art forms. You will note in the following pages that some of the finest art museums in America were established by women. Others had collections compiled by women, who played an important part in their attaining world caliber.

Amelia and Eleanor Hewitt: Cooper-Hewitt Museum

These New York sisters and heiresses used their personal collections and those of their family to create in 1897 the Cooper-Hewitt Museum, the first public museum devoted to decorative arts. In the museum's early years, the sisters managed all operations themselves, running the museum with their own money and the contributions of other women, including Mrs. William Tilden Blodgett. However, when John Pierpont Morgan increased the museum's value enormously by providing it with one of the nation's finest medieval tapestry collections, a male associate of the sisters decided that it was time for a male board to assume the directorship. The sisters fought for several years to avoid losing the management of the Cooper-Hewitt but eventually consented in 1907. This scenario of women initiating cultural institutions, only to lose them to men when the collections became valuable, has been repeated time and again throughout America's history (McCarthy, 1991, pp. 76–77).

Isabella Stewart Gardner: Fenway Court

Isabella Stewart Gardner was an exception to this rule. A flamboyant individualist, Gardner established what is regarded as one of the finest art museums in the country: Boston's Fenway Court. The institution opened its doors to the public in 1903, and Gardner maintained control over the management throughout her lifetime. Long after her death, Gardner's wishes have remained in effect due to a leveraged bequest. The management of the museum and its contents will pass to Harvard University if any collection of paintings other than her own is exhibited or if there is a change in the furniture or permanent displays.

Gardner faced many of the same barriers to giving that women encounter today. Although she exercised control over the management of Fenway Court, she was obsessed with the possibility of becoming poor, despite her vast wealth. Gardner represented the class of women who marry or inherit money that is managed by male financial advisers or is subject to numerous restrictions. Because these women typically play a passive role in managing or increasing the inheritance, they tend to regard the fortune as finite. This often leads to a strong sense of insecurity as the women age. Nonetheless, Isabella Gardner's estate was valued at her death at $9 million, and all but a fraction was invested in Fenway Court (McCarthy, 1991, pp. 149–176).

Gertrude Vanderbilt Whitney: Whitney Museum

A troubled marriage helped lead Gertrude Vanderbilt Whitney to cultural philanthropy. Although the marriage merged two of the wealthiest families in New York City in 1896, Whitney's husband was the epitome of dilettantism, reveling in the kind of life highlighted by F. Scott Fitzgerald. Gertrude Whitney tried at first to please and amuse her husband but ultimately decided that life was more than a merry-go-round of parties.

Following the pattern of her class, Whitney involved herself in her family and in charitable activities. She became a member of the board of Mary Simkhovitch's Greenwich House, funding and overseeing art classes for Irish, Italian, and African immigrants. This experience led to sculpture lessons for herself, and against her family's wishes, she began making a very successful career of her art.

She also collected works by American artists. By 1929 she had amassed six hundred pieces, which she sought to donate to the Metropolitan Museum of Art. The Met's response, however, was that it already had too many American pieces. So in 1931, Gertrude Vanderbilt Whitney founded her own museum, the Whitney Museum of American Art (McCarthy, 1991, pp. 215–244).

Abby Aldrich Rockefeller: Museum of Modern Art

Three quite different women founded the Museum of Modern Art (MOMA) in New York City in 1929: Abby Aldrich Rockefeller, Lillie Bliss, and Mary Quinn Sullivan. Rockefeller and Bliss were the most active. Although the museum was managed by a board of men, the inspiration and energy behind the board were provided by these three women founders, who exercised control in the subtle ways that women have learned over the centuries to gently get their way.

Abby Rockefeller, with her great enthusiasm and dedication,

was MOMA's true nucleus. Not only did she provide ongoing advice and support, but her gifts of money and art in the 1930s kept the museum alive and vital. Besides modern art, Rockefeller also collected American folk art, which she later gave to Williamsburg, Virginia, where the collection is now known as the Abby Aldrich Rockefeller Collection.

Lillie Bliss, in another early leveraged gift, bequeathed her magnificent collection of impressionist and postimpressionist paintings to MOMA with the stipulation that the museum be sufficiently endowed to receive it. This animated the trustees, who despite the Depression raised the necessary $1 million. The Museum of Modern Art was founded on the principle of helping young artists, American artists, and women artists. The first two goals were served admirably, but apart from Georgia O'Keeffe, women artists never fared as well as men in exhibition (McCarthy, 1991, pp. 196–212, 244).

Louisine Havemeyer: Metropolitan Museum of Art

With the encouragement of her friend, the impressionist painter Mary Cassatt, Louisine Havemeyer put together one of the country's greatest collections of nineteenth-century French painting. Havemeyer willed the collection to the Metropolitan Museum of Art in 1929, and that collection alone is considered key in having made the museum the world-class institution it is today.

Havemeyer's husband, Henry, known for his aggressive business style, was also a collector and a benefactor of the arts. Following his death in 1907, Louisine Havemeyer became an ardent feminist and was arrested outside the White House in 1919 during a suffrage rally. In protest, she chose to serve three days in jail rather than pay the bail.

Havemeyer's feminism did not inspire her to advocate on behalf of women artists, even her friend Cassatt. And unlike Isabella Stewart Gardner, Havemeyer did not call for any kind of recognition

in her bequest, even though she gave what may be the single greatest gift ever made to a museum. Her will read modestly, "I have
made very few stipulations in my will in regard to the placing or
care of the collection because I believe there are those who are as
intelligent and as interested as I in the care and conservation of a
valuable gift." It was apparently not her style to demand or leverage, but had she been encouraged to do so, there might have been
earlier recognition of the importance of women artists, and women
might have served on the museum's board well before the 1950s
(Kimmelman, 1993).

Alice Tully: Lincoln Center

Alice Tully gave $4.5 million to underwrite Chamber Music Hall
in New York's Lincoln Center. Heiress to the Corning Glass fortune, Tully originally wanted the gift to be anonymous but was dis-
suaded by no less than John D. Rockefeller III, who encouraged her
to resist her modesty. Tully's philanthropy resulted in improvements
to the concert hall on behalf of its audiences. After looking at the
plans for the hall, she persuaded the designers to make the interior
colors softer and more intimate so as to create a more comfortable
environment in which to listen to music (Bergan, 1992).

Elizabeth Penn Sprague Coolidge: Music

Her passion was music, and Elizabeth Penn Sprague Coolidge was
a pianist accomplished enough to play with the Chicago Symphony.
After her father's death in 1915, she and her mother gave Sprague
Hall, a music building, to Yale University in his memory. Coolidge's
philanthropy always focused on music, but she was also mindful
of the needs of people; in 1925 she established a pension fund for
the Chicago Symphony. Because she wanted to support new musi-
cal efforts and composers as well, she created a foundation to build

an auditorium for chamber music for the Library of Congress. With the opening of the auditorium, she began commissioning compositions from Howard Hanson, Igor Stravinsky, and Sergei Prokofiev, along with many others, including several works for Martha Graham's dance troupe. In 1932 she created the Elizabeth Sprague Coolidge Medal for "eminent service to chamber music" (McHenry, 1980a, p. 79).

Educational Institutions

Education was a priority for many early women philanthropists, who not only helped establish schools and colleges for women but also gave generously to male institutions. These gifts were not always cherished or recognized, however, as in the case of a private midwestern university that knowingly erased all public acknowledgment of a large and very significant bequest made by a female earlier in this century, when the school was all male. The university obtained from this woman an immense gift that helped it become competitive with others of its size by providing a building for a dental school. The woman's name had been inscribed on the building, but forty years later, when more money was needed for an even larger medical complex, this important donor's name was chiseled off the building and replaced by the subsequent donor's.

Other women have believed so fervently in the concept of equitable access to education that they created, raised money for, and donated to the formation of such schools as Emma Willard, Mount Holyoke, and Radcliffe, to name a few. Prior to the Civil War, the only institution of higher education that permitted female enrollment was Ohio's Oberlin College. Women's education proved fertile ground for female philanthropists and fundraisers. Curiously, much of the support that these women garnered was not for the cause of coeducation but rather to keep women's education outside the revered halls of the traditional male bastions. Harvard and

Amherst were equally unwilling to open their doors to women and therefore strongly supported the opening of Smith and Wellesley (Boas, 1971, pp. 233–236).

Margaret Olivia Slocum Sage: Emma Willard School

Margaret Olivia Slocum Sage attended Emma Willard College, and her dedication to her alma mater was apparent when in 1910 she gave money to build a new campus and converted the old campus into a college for female vocational education. This gift constitutes one of the largest individual charitable donations ever made in American history, and the college was eventually the recipient of $1 million from Margaret Sage. Her sizable inheritance came from her husband, Russell Sage, who was not noted for his philanthropy. Nonetheless, after his death in 1907, she established a foundation devoted to solving social problems in his name with an endowment of $10 million. She also named the college after her husband.

By her death in 1918, she had given away $80 million in fulfillment of her philosophy that women were responsible for the moral progress of civilization. Institutions such as Harvard, Yale, the Tuskegee Institute, the YWCA and YMCA, the Woman's Hospital of New York, and many cultural organizations were the recipients of her magnanimity (McHenry, 1980b, pp. 363–364).

Sophia Smith: Smith College

Sophia Smith became deaf at the age of forty. Her first educational gift, after inheriting a fortune twenty-five years later, was to endow a school for deaf-mutes in Northampton, Massachusetts. Later Smith followed her pastor's advice to found a women's college, although the presidents of Williams and Yale tried to dissuade her (McCarthy, 1991, p. 175). By 1870, the year she died, she had bequeathed more than $393,000 to Smith College. It opened five years later, with fourteen students (McHenry, 1980b, p. 276).

Lydia Moss Bradley: Bradley University

A shrewd businesswoman and successful real estate developer, Lydia Moss Bradley managed and increased the value of the estate left to her at her husband's death in 1867. The couple had begun plans to endow a major educational institution in memory of their six children, all of whom had died as infants. Bradley saw the dream become reality when the first buildings for Bradley Polytechnic Institute were erected in 1897. Due to Lydia Bradley's influence, the college became a pioneer in the field of domestic science (McHenry, 1980b, p. 48).

Emma Carola Woerishoffer: Bryn Mawr College

Emma Carola Woerishoffer lived only twenty-six years, but her highly developed belief in the value of public service led her to bequeath $750,000 to Bryn Mawr College to improve its training of women for public and social service. This bequest resulted in the first graduate department of social work in the United States (Fisher, 1993, pp. 16–17). Woerishoffer, who came from a New York publishing family, also devoted many volunteer hours to the public good. Like Anne Tracy Morgan, daughter of J. Pierpont Morgan, she supported the women shirtwaist workers in their strike of 1909 (McHenry, 1980b, p. 291).

Mary Elizabeth Garrett: Johns Hopkins University and Bryn Mawr School

The daughter of the founder of the Baltimore and Ohio Railroad, Mary Elizabeth Garrett inherited in 1884, at the age of thirty, a large portion of her father's estate. Not only did she give to Bryn Mawr College, but in 1885 she also contributed to the establishment of Philadelphia's Bryn Mawr School, intended to prepare young women for college in the same ways as their male counterparts were being trained in traditional preparatory schools.

Garrett's most laudable gift, however, has become the leveraged one she made to Johns Hopkins Medical School. To help the college succeed in its lagging fundraising efforts, she offered to give $350,000 of the necessary $500,000 if women were admitted to the medical school and allowed to follow the same program as men. By placing these restrictions, lately known as "opportunities," on her gift, she opened up medical education to women (Fisher, 1993, pp. 14–15).

Anita McCormick Blaine: University of Chicago

Anita McCormick's mother, Nettie, always encouraged philanthropy in her children. After Anita grew up, married, and was widowed only three years later, the education of her young son became her focus of attention. As she had not enjoyed her own tutored education, she was determined that her son would have something better. Feeling that teachers were authoritarian and did not encourage self-discovery, she consulted with Jane Addams and others about a new model of school. Together they proposed an education that would be more adaptive to the times and would stimulate children to learn about social responsibility. In 1901, Blaine gave $1 million in property and assets to the University of Chicago's school of education to help promote this dream (McCarthy, 1982, pp. 112–116).

Elizabeth Pitts Merrill-Palmer: Merrill-Palmer Institute of Human Development and Family Life

The socialization of women at the turn of the twentieth century and an innate nurturing instinct were influential in the values and vision of Elizabeth Pitts Merrill-Palmer. After inheriting money from her father and her husband, Merrill-Palmer acted on her belief that the quality of motherhood affects the quality of a community. In 1916 she bequeathed $3 million to establish Detroit's Merrill-Palmer School for Motherhood and Home Training (subsequently called the Merrill-Palmer Institute of Human Development and Family Life). The school was a nursery that also trained women for motherhood and later included the training of fathers for fatherhood as well. It is interesting to note that Merrill-Palmer gave the school not only her husband's name but her own family name as well (Fisher, 1993, p. 18).

Other Women Contributing to Education

Many other women also contributed significant fortunes to education (McHenry, 1980b):

- Journalist and publishing heiress Ellen Browning Scripps established, with her brother, the Scripps Institute of Oceanography at the University of California. She also founded Scripps College for Women in 1927 and contributed to the founding of the San Diego Zoo.

- Josephine Louise Le Monnier Newcomb was an astute businesswoman whose only child, Harriott Sophie Newcomb, died in 1870 at age fifteen. Newcomb, who had previously given large donations to Washington and Lee University, gave $1 million in memory of her daughter to Tulane University in New Orleans for the H. Sophie Newcomb Memorial College for women. In her will she bequeathed an additional $2.5 million to the college.

- Phoebe Apperson Hearst attended public schools and received training as a teacher before marrying George Hearst, whose mining holdings and publishing empire are legendary. Following her husband's death in 1891, she began making large gifts to the University of California at Berkeley, earmarked for several purposes, including women's scholarships, several buildings, archaeological expeditions, and a museum. She also supported the establishment and organization of an anthropology department. Always interested in teaching, she financed a training school for kindergarten teachers in 1897.

- Mary Porter Tileston Hemenway supported many institutions, including Wellesley College and the Tuskegee and Hampton Institutes, along with programs beginning in 1876 that introduced American history into the public school curriculum.

- Mary Gwendolin Caldwell founded the National Catholic School of Philosophy and Theology with the stipulation that she be known as the founder. In 1887 the school opened as the Catholic University of America in the District of Columbia.

- Sarah Anne Worthington King Peter founded the Cincinnati Protestant Orphan Asylum. After her first husband's death, she remarried and moved to Philadelphia, where in 1848 she began the Philadelphia School of Design, the first school of industrial arts in America.

More Worthy Women and Their Philanthropy

Although education has been a primary focus for women philanthropists throughout American history, other causes have benefited from women's giving as well. From pioneer settlements to women's suffrage, from historic preservation to the environment, women have been involved from the start.

Doña Patricia de la Garza de León: Victoria, Texas

Marriage usually shaped the lives of wealthy women in the eighteenth century because they generally stood to gain by a "good marriage" to a prosperous man. But Doña Patricia de la Garza de León was an exception to the rule. One of the earliest pioneer women to settle in Texas, it was her $10,000 inheritance that helped her husband found the town of Victoria in 1824. When he died nine years later, she was the richest woman in Texas and used her considerable means to create educational, religious, and cultural community institutions that lived on long after her death (Winegarten, 1986, p. 10).

Carrie Chapman Catt: Women's Suffrage and the League of Women Voters

The closing of Carrie Chapman Catt's commencement address at Iowa State College in 1921 typifies her life of giving fully to a righteous cause. She challenged graduating students to live their lives as she had hers: "To the wrongs that need resistance, to the right that needs assistance, to the future in the distance, give yourselves." She dedicated her life to involving women in the political process, educating voters, and promoting world peace. Always active in the suffrage movement, she inspired others to give to help women achieve the vote. In 1892 she sold her sapphire jewelry to provide funds to establish the League of Women Voters. Publishing entrepreneur Miriam Florence Folline Leslie left Catt her estate of nearly $1 million in 1914 to further women's suffrage (McHenry, 1980a, pp. 243–244).

Catt's alma mater, Iowa State University, and its alumni and friends have recently honored her by creating the Carrie Chapman Catt Center for Women and Politics. Following a $5 million renovation, the center will be housed in a nineteenth-century campus building to be renamed Carrie Chapman Catt Hall. Iowa State is paying tribute to one woman's contribution at the same time as it is encouraging more female giving for the project. Just as Catt challenged those graduating seniors, Iowa State is challenging alumnae and women all over America to endow the center's operation. Appropriately, it has established the Sapphire Club to recognize major donors of $25,000 or more. Contributors will receive a star sapphire necklace or pin designed exclusively for this club.

Historic Preservation

Saving George Washington's home, Mount Vernon, was the first historic preservation project in the nation, and it was inspired and funded by women. Ann Pamela Cunningham's mother visited the home in 1853 and found it shabby and neglected. In a letter to her daughter in South Carolina, she suggested that women do something about the sad state of affairs "if the men could not do it." The preservation of the building and land through the Mount Vernon Ladies Association became Cunningham's passion until her death in 1874. She was aided by the Virginia actress Anna Cora Mowatt Ritchie (Wamsley and Cooper, 1976, pp. 151–156).

Twenty-eight years later, it was Texan Clara Driscoll's first philanthropic gift that saved San Antonio's Alamo from destruction. The daughter of a wealthy south Texas rancher, she became a generous donor who at her death left her entire fortune to establish a children's hospital in Corpus Christi (Winegarten, 1986).

Former *Chicago Tribune* women's editor Ruth De Young Kohler, originally from Wisconsin, began restoring an inn in Greenbush, Wisconsin, dating back to the mid 1800s in memory of her sister-in-law, Marie Kohler. The Wade House and lands surrounding it were dedicated in 1954 and are today one of the seven historic sites owned by the State Historical Society of Wisconsin (Chase, 1971, pp. 4–12). Ruth Kohler's family remains a strong financial supporter of the site, and her daughter, Ruth De Young Kohler II, carries on the tradition of philanthropy established by her mother with her support of the Michael Kohler Art Center in Sheboygan, Wisconsin, and her gifts to women's causes.

When Savannah's Old City Market was converted to a parking lot in 1955, seven Savannah women organized the Historic Savannah Foundation. Cofounder Katherine J. Clark led the campaign to restore the district and became the driving force in the rescue of downtown Savannah. The last of the seven women, Clark died in 1993, but she lived to see Savannah attract hundreds of thousands of tourists each year to its restored historic district ("Katherine J. Clark," 1993).

Conservation

An early champion of Wisconsin's natural environment, Wilhelmine Tiefenthaeler La Budde promoted reforestation. She began school conservation programs and encouraged the establishment of school forests in the state, in which students could practice what they learned about conservation. Her greatest contribution, however, was the donation of a major portion of the Horicon Marsh Wildlife Area in the 1930s to help create the thirty-one-thousand-acre refuge, which is referred to as the "Everglades of the North" (*Famous Wisconsin Women*, 1972, pp. 17–24).

A Conclusion and a Challenge

At the end of the eighteenth century, some two hundred relief societies were being supported by wealthy women. During the next century, more than four hundred settlement homes were set up and maintained. Each of these six hundred-plus organizations had at least fifteen women actively supporting them with their time and money. That means at least nine thousand women in the first two centuries of our nation's history were involved in philanthropy and made impressive contributions affecting hundreds of thousands of lives. Yet most of these women are virtually unknown.

Preeminent women's historian Gerda Lerner says in her book *The Female Experience* (1992, p. 192):

What is important here is not only the scattered activity of small groups of women, which has remained unnoticed and generally neglected. More important is the suggestion of a developmental pattern of community building, whereby the early infrastructure is created and maintained through the voluntary association of women, who then proceed to institution building. Frequently, such institutions, once established, become "businesses" or are taken over by the community as public institutions. In either case, they are then headed by a man and led by corporate trustees, usually also men. Once institutions have reached that stage, they are noted as "existing" by historians.

In the last decades of the twentieth century, women are again exercising their philanthropic clout in the growing numbers of women's funds and the other causes they support. A major difference this time is the publicizing of their efforts, efforts that are now more often directed toward change, not just charity.

Continuing the Philanthropic Tradition

Looking back on our ten predictions for women's philanthropy, it is apparent that some are already becoming fact. The historical women philanthropists profiled in this chapter were extraordinary primarily in that they were women who controlled the disbursement of their own wealth and used it to improve society. In the last few decades of the twentieth century, more and more women have taken control of their financial resources, and nonprofit institutions and organizations large and small have responded by developing giving programs targeting women. Many executives of nonprofit organizations also recognize that these programs will not succeed without leadership programs to involve women in decision-making roles as board and committee members, foundation and corporation executives, development officers, and volunteer fundraisers. Many women, meanwhile, are not content to wait for the traditional nonprofits to come around. They have established women's funds and political action committees to raise money for causes important to women.

Nonprofit organizations must begin to study the motivations, attitudes, and giving patterns of their major women donors and publish their findings. In so doing, they will not only help set the record straight as to women's contributions to society but will also establish role models and higher standards for up-and-coming women philanthropists.

Chapter Three

Voices of Women Philanthropists

In this chapter we profile eight women who are representative of the kind of advocacy philanthropist who is just now coming into her own. These women are not generalizations of female philanthropists; they speak only for themselves. Yet their individuality is at once unique to each and common to them all. All eight are accessible, intelligent, warm, and innovative, and they have a great passion for life, change, giving, and making a difference. They have confronted inequities and injustice in life and have overcome them. They are bold enough to dream their dreams and make them come true.

We single out these women because we believe that their stories and efforts can both inspire others and enlighten development officers. Because women's stories have seldom been heard or their experiences documented in any detail, we are pleased to be able to do so here. On these pages you will see how these women were inspired in philanthropy, why they have chosen the causes they support, and how they view volunteerism, women, relationships, money, and power.

Few of these women had female philanthropic role models or mentors. Fortunately, however, the increasing numbers of women like them ensure that this will not be the case for future generations. We hope that these stories will provide insight into the motivations and successes of these brave and resourceful women, as well as some ideas for development officers about how to approach women as donors. These leaders will serve as voices for countless thousands around the nation who are either giving now or are ready to do so.

Maddie Levitt

Des Moines, Iowa

Maddie Levitt is a dynamo. Something always seems on the verge of happening with Maddie, and it usually does. She has a fresh optimism tempered with hard-driving realism, and she knows exactly when to give one or the other the upper hand. Maddie loves to shop and dresses in bright designer clothing. She drives a custom-designed Volkswagen around her hometown of Des Moines, Iowa.

We first became acquainted when she was recommended as a person who might be interested in discussing women's giving, even possibly in funding an organization to encourage women as philanthropists. So on Mother's Day weekend in 1992, we traveled to Des Moines. Maddie graciously showed us around town, and it soon became apparent that everyone knew her—not as someone born to wealth, though that she was, but as a regular person who cared a great deal about her community and worked hard for it. Whether we were at the country club or the local diner, Maddie spoke to everyone and inquired with genuine interest about their lives.

When it came time to talk business about our need for an organization, the other Maddie emerged and asked some really tough questions. Remembering that conversation, Maddie says, "I was flattered and excited because I felt that the whole concept of recognizing women and philanthropy was something long overdue, and no one had ever asked me to do anything. I am so curious to see what will happen to this."

After more negotiation and a meeting of six senior development officers at the annual assembly of the Council for the Advancement and Support of Education (CASE) in Atlanta, Maddie became part of our dream. She offered to give $100,000 over

four years to start up the organization, which ultimately became the
National Network on Women as Philanthropists (NNWP), now
part of the School of Family Resources and Consumer Sciences at
the University of Wisconsin, Madison.

Unlike many women of her generation (she was born in 1924)
and status, Maddie chose to work outside the home after years of
full-time volunteer work. Her first paid job was with the United
Way, where she had long been a volunteer fundraiser. When asked
to take a six-week temporary position in public relations, Maddie
accepted and ended up staying more than eight years. Following
that, she worked on the development staff for two hospitals before
moving on to Drake University.

Maddie is currently finishing her fifth year as the volunteer
national chair of the $115 million Campaign for Drake. Her own
donations represented the first gift the campaign received ($2.4 mil-
lion) and a challenge gift of $3 million, which Maddie promised in
the fall of 1992, provided that the university raised another $12 mil-
lion by the summer of 1993. The successful campaign, which raised
$131 million ($16 million over the original goal), concluded in
1992. She particularly likes challenge gifts and has certainly proved
their effectiveness with the Drake campaign.

> I think challenge gifts act as an incentive. When I was asked to serve
> as the national chair, I thought about it long and hard and knew I
> had to do something that would challenge the board of governors
> and trustees to raise their philanthropic sights. Of course, many had
> never been asked before. But I knew that to present this to others,
> I had first to give myself. That's when I gave the three-million-dol-
> lar gift which, forty-five days later, had generated twenty-six million
> dollars, more than had ever been raised for a capital campaign at
> Drake. And that money came from seventy-one people on those two
> boards.

It is easy to see that her title of national chair was not merely symbolic. Maddie worked. As the first woman to chair a college fundraising campaign of over $100 million, she traveled more than two hundred thousand miles around the United States and Canada asking for money. To use her time wisely, she made only calls asking for $100,000 or more, although she admits that she did not always get that amount or any gift at all. As for refusals, she did not take them personally. "I used to get very upset with people, especially physicians, who could give but didn't. However, as I matured, I felt I couldn't spend my time worrying about those people," she said.

Maddie's high degree of confidence should be a motivation for other women who are volunteer fundraisers. Sitting across the desk from the great many men she asked for money, Maddie felt herself their equal and nothing less, a trait she credits to the respect she always had from her father. She also traces this feeling of equality to being a major player in the campaign herself and having a sincere belief in the value of the university. "They knew I didn't have to be running around the United States asking for money," she says. Such honesty and self-esteem are what make Maddie so effective. She understands the issues of money and power and is not ashamed to make them work for herself and her causes.

One of Maddie's finest efforts, in her estimation, was using an all-female fundraising committee to collect $3.4 million to restore Old Main, the oldest building on campus. She recalls becoming interested in the project through the combined appeal of the community, the old building's extraordinary acoustics, and the challenge of showing the primarily male fundraising committee that women can raise money too.

> I found that women wanted to be a part of things but separate from their husbands. Every single one of the women on the committee was married, but none of their husbands' names appear on the plaque inside the building. There were eighteen women in all, and very few had done fundraising before, but they were delighted to be

asked for themselves, not their husbands, and to be able to make a commitment to something that they felt was very important to the community. It made them feel extremely independent. I handpicked them, so I knew they each had outside incomes; I knew the cast of characters, and they realized that they had to give first. Most had never raised a penny for Drake and for the most part hadn't given either. Not all were even graduates. First, I called individually on each committee member and then had a luncheon to lay out the campaign, which took six months to complete. We didn't ask them to do a lot—maybe five or six calls, and always with someone else. It helped a lot to have the president's support for this, and he made it a very high priority in the capital funds campaign.

Actually, Maddie enjoys one of the most supportive bases for women and philanthropy that we have encountered on any campus in the United States. Drake's vice president for institutional advancement, Jack Ohle, could have been suspicious of our interests in Maddie and the fact that she was giving the NNWP money, but he bowled us over with his enthusiasm. On our first visit to Des Moines, in 1992, we had spoken for only a short time before Ohle was planning a conference with the newly forming NNWP to be held on the Drake campus. He is a mixture of pragmatism and idealism and understands, as Maddie does, the opportunities presented by the combination of women, money, and power. He knows that it will pay off in the long run and is self-confident enough to allow that to happen.

Maddie is a graduate of Ohio State University; her Drake roots come from her father, Ellis Levitt, formerly a member of the university's board of trustees. He had turned a family consumer finance business into a billion-dollar company before selling to Norwest Corporation in 1982 for $232 million. Life had not always been so affluent for the family, however. Maddie's grandfather was a peddler who came to Des Moines from Lithuania with nothing but a pack on his back before beginning his loan business at the turn of the twentieth century. Maddie credits him for her cheerful ability to accept and deal with life as it is. She recalls, "My grandfather had a ring with an arrow pointing up on one side and down on the other. When everything in life was going well, he would turn the arrow down to show that adversity can happen, and when things were going badly, he would turn it up to show that things will look up."

But Maddie's father was the primary spur to her philanthropic interests. He set up trusts for Maddie and her brother when they were in their teens. According to Maddie, her father established separate trusts because he knew that the two would have individual interests. This has proved to be the case: her brother supports mainly the arts and medicine, while she gives to human services and higher education. Both, however, have led major university capital campaigns: he headed the University of Iowa's $150 million fundraising campaign at the same time that Maddie was chairing Drake's campaign. Maddie has adopted her father's approach and set up separate trusts for her three children and four grandchildren.

Always somewhat different from her peers, Maddie worked outside the home when other women of her age and means were playing bridge and traveling. However, she says, not until after her divorce in 1987 did she become stronger and more independent. As with many women, a significant life event was the catalyst that forced her to take action. "I have become much more self-confident and learned a whole lot about myself since then. Like many other women, I always relied heavily on the decision making of my spouse and didn't assert myself regarding philanthropy, even though it was my family's money. For years I missed out on the fun of seeing what my money could do for my interests."

Maddie has inner resources that many of us can only wish for. The inspiration of her father, her own power and confidence, her ability to reflect and learn, and her indomitable spirit of well-being are surely major factors pointing to why this petite dynamo has been able to realize her potential as a philanthropist and volunteer fundraiser.

Harriet Denison
Portland, Oregon

Harriet Denison was to participate with us in a program on women and philanthropy at a monthly meeting of the Portland chapter of the National Society of Fundraising Executives (NSFRE). We met her just before the meeting. For nearly two hours, this very intelligent and committed woman described how much she was enjoying managing her family's foundation.

Harriet is from a fairly conservative family but has always been a bit of a rebel. Following her graduation from college, she joined the Peace Corps and taught in Tanzania for two years. After returning to the United States, she married and spent two years traveling, much of that time on a sailboat in Mexico and California.

Although Harriet's father supported conservative Republican organizations, he was unusually broad-minded about his daughter's life and choices. She said that he was very careful not to pass on his prejudices. Rather than veto her ideas, he "played the devil's advocate for anything I wanted to do. He was always very concerned, but in a parental way. Not wanting to put something in my way, but just making sure I had thought it through." As for her stint in Tanzania, Harriet acknowledged, he never said anything outright, but he was scared to death. Both of her parents were generally supportive of what she wanted to do, and according to Harriet, "I've done some very strange things by their standards."

The family foundation came about as a result of investments made by her maternal grandfather, Ralph L. Smith, in lumber and West Coast timberlands. "He did do some good things, which I think were because of the influence of my grandmother, who donated quite a bit of money to black colleges. That was in the fifties, before it was an acceptable thing to do." Upon her grandfather's death, the foundation came under the control of his three children: Harriet's mother in Portland, her aunt in Kansas City, and her uncle in Los Angeles. By mutual consent, the trustees each donated money to their own local interest groups. The foundation now has assets of $16 million, which means that each trustee can allocate approximately $266,000 annually.

In 1986, after twenty years of trusteeship, Harriet's mother, Margaret, asked her daughter to take over responsibility for her share. Margaret had been a major inspiration for Harriet through her early interest in women and children's programs. Through Harriet's efforts, the Ralph L. Smith Foundation has provided start-up funds and continuing support for the Women's Foundation of Oregon. Unquestionably, the Women's Foundation is Harriet's greatest love; she created it and continues to be involved. In fact, one might say that she had been preparing for this for much of her life.

We asked Harriet about some of her strongest commitments, and diversity emerged in first place—no doubt a result of her finely honed sense of justice, a trait she may have learned from her grandmother. Harriet is personally committed to diversity within the women's foundation; as she explains, "For the first two or three years, that was what we were doing: creating diversity by building trust and investment from other women's communities outside the white middle-class women in the foundation. When we recruit board members, we make it very clear that they are expected to put in a lot of time on diversity. As a result, every time new board members come on, we get stronger and stronger."

In fundraising, too, Harriet believes that diversity is an asset. She claims that often in organizations, the white women do all the fundraising, and there is resentment on all sides. But that is not what happens on this board. "We team women up who complement one another with experience or whatever else is needed so that it's a stronger team." She observes that women of color want to raise money just like other women and that effectiveness depends on motivation, not pigmentation. And Harriet is firmly convinced that women *are* motivated to raise money: "Anybody who hasn't raised money in an organization such as this is dying to learn," she averred. When we raised our eyebrows in disbelief, she said, "Really, they believe in the cause and want to learn how to do it."

Addressing the matter of diversity in another way, Harriet shared the awkwardness of being a wealthy woman who has little or no contact with people of other cultures and classes. "It's difficult for me. But I do it because it's important to have a window to what is happening in the world. Many women, especially older women, have never had the experience of an equal relationship with people outside their class and culture," she says. She feels that this limits people as they look at ways to be philanthropic. "Until women get some feel for the unfairness of a lot of the systems that have been set up that benefit them and put them in positions of privilege and will be threatened if things are changed, they can't really understand what's needed and be willing to do something about it."

Harriet passionately advocates that women educate themselves in money matters and take control of their own finances. Relating a story about a woman in her sixties, Harriet said, "She was very pleased because at last she was put on the board of trustees of her own trust. Sixty years old and she's just now getting to the point where she can have a little sway over her own money." She noted that even her own mother had to have a "significant event" occur, her father's death, to become comfortable dealing with money.

An introspective and reflective person, Harriet has had to come to grips with being a woman of wealth in a grassroots organization. The issue of money and power came up again and again in our conversation, and we sense that she is not yet comfortable with the subject but continues to search for ways to explain and define her role.

I am very aware of my privilege, and because I have had the time and money, I have been able to be involved in personal growth education. Through this, I became aware of my ability to create change. But what had to go along with that is a sensitivity to power, so I don't abuse it. I'm probably more aware of the issues around power than some people. It's a real balance. You are depriving society if you don't use the power that you have, but you have to use it ethically, so you don't abuse it and become referred to as "that woman with all of the money who wants to control everything." Where I am now with the foundation is really around the issue of power. I am the founder, I am a major donor, and I am responsible for the major donations due the foundation. In spite of who I am, what I say, what I think, and what I feel about whether or not I want to control the organization, it can't help but influence the other people in the organization, particularly when I am in the room. My feeling is that now it's under way, and it isn't just my organization. But as long as I'm physically there, I'm going to be an influence. . . . I think more study needs to be done about the whole issue of power and how it is abused and used ethically, which is really the issue.

Referring to herself as a "developing philanthropist," Harriet is very aware of her obligation to establish credibility by financially supporting an organization before asking others for gifts. In fact, she strongly believes that if she gives more to the Women's Foundation, this will in turn encourage others to give larger amounts.

Although she would no doubt shudder to be referred to as a libertarian, Harriet is not fond of large institutions or organizations and feels that they do not get to the root of the problems but only deal with direct services.

What I give to is social change. Until somebody pays attention to changing what is causing homelessness, what is causing girls to run away, what is causing AIDS in women—until somebody pays attention—these things will go on and continue to grow. I am interested in the real change and aware of how much money and how much work needs to be put into it before things happen. But I think it is a very good use of money because here's where empowerment comes in. If I can do something as a donor, like giving money to a group of people who are themselves going to make the change, I think it's a whole lot different from giving it to an agency that makes people totally dependent.

Harriet Denison is clearly a woman who has been able to accept her numerous advantages in life and, in so doing, put them to use with her experience and values. She is an emerging philanthropist, and one can only wonder at how much she has already accomplished and her larger potential to educate and motivate others.

Jo Moore

Wilmette, Illinois

Jo Moore walked into Chicago's Palmer House one fall afternoon, looking very much the young suburban baby boomer matron—in this case, one with a law degree. Not many suburban matrons, however, would be able to share the following story only a few minutes into the conversation.

I was the oldest of three daughters and ended up working in a meat-packing plant. My dad knew the man who owned the plant, but the fact is, I am the only woman I've ever known socially who was actually a member of the meatpackers union, and that's unbelievably difficult work and difficult conditions. Women were segregated to the lowest-paying jobs with the least security. When I talked about this with older women, I was hassled by the union. I can't help but tell you, those experiences made me who I am today. I worry about this for my children and try to talk to them and get them around a lot, but the truth is, they live very different lives than I did.

Growing up in Minneapolis and attending integrated Catholic schools, which included Native Americans as students, Jo had the view of the real world that Harriet Denison feels she missed. "I think it really made me much more aware and empathetic with people who come from different backgrounds and different classes. Even though I lived in a strongly middle-class family, a lot of the kids I went to school with did not." Although no longer a practicing Catholic, Jo credits her Catholic education—"the years of liberation theology"—for both her philanthropic endeavors and her community activism.

Jo Moore's family also had a strong influence on her philanthropic values. Her mother focused on contributing to her large family (Jo has forty-five first cousins), and her father is a volunteer fundraiser for a benefit golf tournament, which has raised up to $120,000 a year for a center for the hearing-impaired. "He went there because of a niece who was using some of their services and found out that they needed a van, so he started the golf tournament to buy the van," Jo proudly relates. Even today, Jo's father is involved in raising money for the heart institute of a hospital where a friend of his had triple bypass surgery, and he is starting another golf tournament for the hospice at the hospital where Jo's mother died in 1989.

But Jo credits her husband's brother as being the role model for them. She says, "My husband's brother, Rob Moore, began to trade at the Chicago Board of Trade a year before we moved to Chicago. He quickly became a very successful trader and was just as quick to become a generous model to various charities. He truly was a role model for us."

This family clearly gets involved in things that touch them personally, and Jo uses this philosophy when approaching people for money.

> As a fundraiser, I always try to figure out what moves people. Maybe they have a personal reason, such as being abused in a first marriage. Maybe they want to be on a board or learn volunteering skills that they can't get elsewhere. You certainly can find happiness and reward in giving for whatever reason you are getting involved. I'm

thrilled when they do, especially if it's something I am passionate about. For myself, I know that there are similar branches to be shaken. I don't think it is unusual. I have a strong sense of justice, and it's great fun for me to be able to actually cause change by writing a check. That's about the most fun way I can spend my money.

We asked Jo which of her other branches could be shaken, and she mentioned her support of women's causes as a result of experiences in both the workforce and the education system. "I'm not interested in supporting even my law school. It was a struggle being a woman there, and women received no affirmations. I had a baby in the middle of my third year, and only one teacher mentioned it. I had the baby on a Friday night and was back in class the next Thursday. Sometimes I had to bring the baby in a backpack, and no one mentioned it. It was like it never happened," she recalled. As a result of these encounters, Jo has been an active volunteer and contributor to the Chicago Foundation for Women.

After three years of work with a shelter for battered women, Jo says she was ready to be a part of the foundation's first fundraising meeting. "I was really excited to get involved in a women's foundation that would address all of the issues and that hopefully would also educate people about how these issues are all intertwined. There aren't separate problems of domestic violence or decent day care or whatever. All of these are problems with people who are living in difficult situations."

Jo's law background has provided her with a professionalism that she uses in her volunteer work. "I really wanted to take my volunteer work seriously and be professional about it, and so, just as a person generally has only one career at a time, I decided that it would be much more rewarding to devote myself to one area of volunteer work, rather than being on a number of different boards." Consequently, the women's foundation is the only board Jo has served on, and for her it has been a wonderful experience. "This is the moment in time for the women's movement and the women's funding movement. This wonderful train was speeding ahead, and I hopped on."

Jo does not describe either herself or her husband as having come from wealth. When her husband met great success at the Chicago Board of Trade, they were astonished. Still, she feels a part of their success. "If it weren't for the fact that I had the security of a law degree and a law career, my husband would never have taken this wild shot at the Chicago Board of Trade. He is a very conservative guy about finances." In addition, she says, she was "his one-person rooting team." He called her every day at noon and two o'clock so that they could go over all of the trades, and then they talked more at night.

Despite her role in the family finances, Jo still has trouble writing big checks and needs to be encouraged by her husband.

I have my own issues with money because I didn't earn it, although I do strongly feel that we couldn't have made this money if I hadn't thought it was a great idea and advocated it to my husband. I was the one who said, You can do this, and hey, if we lose this money, I'll practice law full time and we'll get all of the money back in a year. Still, he has to encourage me to write bigger checks. He tells me he's giving a certain amount to this cause and thinks I should reconsider the amount I am giving. His point is, if I'm not giving a lot of money when we are making a lot of money, we sure aren't going to be giving a lot when we aren't. But it really is hard for me to write big checks.

She explains that in part her hesitation comes from knowing how hard it would be to make that money again. Also, the family had to make a number of adjustments as it went in one year "from being middle-class to being very not-middle-class." They discussed how to spend the money, what it meant to their children, what kind of example they are setting, how to maintain their values, and how they want to live with a lot of money.

We asked Jo how to address women's lack of confidence about money. "I think you have to talk and talk and talk. Women have to be made to understand that even if they don't work outside the home, they are working within the home, which adds enormous value to the home and the family. You have to get them to believe that and to feel that they have every right to make decisions about where the money is going."

Heading up the major gift committee for the Chicago Foundation for Women, Jo has spent a lot of time considering how to approach women for money, particularly those who are business owners. She recommends posing philanthropy as entrepreneurism. "What better place for women who are successful entrepreneurs to give their money than to an entrepreneurial organization like the Chicago Women's Foundation? We are putting together new little groups and growing them to provide incredible services." She is also hopeful about young professional women, who are now between the ages of thirty and forty-five and believes that as they gain professionally, they are going to revolutionize the nonprofit world and are even now funding most of the change-oriented organizations in the United States. As for older women, Jo is discouraged, at least about their potential for giving to causes like a women's foundation.

> I think the whole thing flies in the face of how they live their lives, what they bought into, and how they view themselves and their relationship to their husbands. Women were taught to be giving, giving, giving all the time but not to do anything for themselves because that's selfish. Women tell us they think it's selfish to have a fund that gives money only to women and girls. But no one else is giving to them, and no one else is suffering more. However, I'm hopeful because women are so generous to everyone else that I can't imagine that when they get money, they won't be generous with it too, especially when they earn it themselves.

It is not surprising that this engaging woman with her well-defined ideas of justice, particularly with regard to women, was heavily involved in supporting women candidates during the 1992 elections. She encouraged others to give the entire amount they would spend on a fall wardrobe to women candidates. We talked about how women of all income levels could in this way give to the causes that were important to them, whether it were six figures for an entire wardrobe or the cost of a single outfit.

On our way back to Madison after the interview, we reflected on the incredible sense of values that this couple had maintained despite their almost overnight ride to riches. Jo Moore has much to be proud of and much to be thankful for, and she serves as an outstanding role model.

Toby Lerner Ansin

Miami, Florida

Miami Beach's Lincoln Road has seen finer days. Despite revival attempts by the city, three decades of neglect still cling to it. This state suits some tenants marvelously, however, because with lower rents than the trendy neighborhoods, they can live but a few blocks from the hotel district, where European designers and American rock stars vie for oceanfront real estate. On any given day, passersby can peer through the large plate-glass storefront windows at 905 Lincoln Road and watch young dancers practicing in what was formerly Bonwit Teller, an upscale women's clothing store. This address is home to the Miami City Ballet, created in the mid 1980s by Toby Lerner Ansin, frustrated ballerina and gifted volunteer fundraiser.

We met Toby in Miami Beach on a scorching, humid day in September over lunch at an art deco café down the street from the ballet. A warm and modest woman, Toby has a naturalness that made us feel we had known her forever, and she is very modest about the fact that almost single-handedly, she established a ballet company that is well on its way to becoming world-class. During a time when other companies have suffered financial droughts and in some cases even closed their doors, the Miami City Ballet has flourished and continues to add to its repertoire while also increasing the length and scope of its season.

Ballet was a passion for Toby in her hometown of Boston until about the age of fourteen, when she decided that she did not have the talent or the technique to become a professional ballerina. Although her parents were both involved in the arts and had supported her ballet efforts, they were relieved when she decided to make dance a hobby rather than a career. But the intensity of her interest in ballet never ended, and this, combined with a most unusual creative sense, prompted Toby to bring dance performances to Miami, where she had moved following her marriage at the age of twenty some three decades ago.

During our conversation, we were struck by the number of times she spoke about creativity. In her own case, she uses her talent to get people's attention and win their support for her project. "I started dance luncheons through my synagogue," she explains, "to introduce temple women to different forms of dance. We started with modern dance and had a modern dancer come in and give a lecture about the history of modern dance, perform modern dance without music and costumes, do the same piece with costumes and music, and then teach a modern dance class to all the women at the luncheon. Then we did it with jazz, tap, flamenco, and ballet."

Eventually Toby was asked to serve on the Dade County Council of Arts and Sciences, giving her the opportunity to act on her interests. In no time, she organized a dance umbrella organization to oversee local companies and help them with venues, publicity, and marketing.

All of what Toby had been doing for more than twenty years was leading up to her meeting Edward Villella, America's greatest male dancer, in May 1985, and meshing her creative interests with his vision of establishing a national ballet company. Looking back on that first meeting, Toby says, "When he thought about this lady who told him, 'In a few months from now we're gonna have a board, we're gonna have a press conference, and we're gonna announce this ballet company,' he must have laughed." But she meant every word she said.

First, Toby called six friends and asked each of them to give $1,000. Her own contribution made $7,000, which she used that summer to fly Villella to Miami to meet the dance, philanthropic, and business communities. A steering committee was in place by the end of the summer, and in October a board of directors was elected.

What gave Toby the courage and knowledge to attempt something as radical as starting a new ballet company? Toby, like Maddie Levitt, chalks it up to a significant life event: in 1984, Toby divorced and began handling her own money. She made some major decisions for herself, ranging from investments to getting the roof redone. "I've grown tremendously during these eight years, in ways I wouldn't have been able to otherwise. On the one hand, it's sort of exhilarating to be able to make all of your own decisions, but on the other hand, I really wasn't prepared to do it." She believes that younger women who have professions and salaries of their own will not have to go through the same kinds of financial ordeals as her generation did.

Ever an optimist, Toby admits that she is somewhat impulsive—but optimism and impulsiveness may both be qualities essential to the creative process. Toby is also grounded in reality, and to counter her impulsiveness, she deliberately surrounds herself with people who "will send me back and not always let me do what my impulse is to do, because sometimes to go slower is faster. And yet, if I didn't occasionally act impulsively, some of the things I've gotten done never would have happened."

As for people who predicted that the ballet would never coalesce, Toby used the same tactic: surrounding herself with those who felt as she did and wanted to make it happen. It did. On October 17, 1986, the curtains went up for the first time on the Miami City Ballet. Looking back on that exhilarating time, her sense of humor is apparent when she remarks, "Edward said we had to have a theater. So I called and reserved the Gusman Theater in my name. People would phone to schedule the theater, and it looked like I was going to perform. So later I said, 'I'll tell you what. Give money to the ballet company, and I won't dance.'"

There is nothing she has not done for the ballet company, and she still fills in whenever she is needed. But fundraising is where her talents lie. Combining her passion for the ballet, her outgoing and gregarious personality, and her willingness to ask, she loves raising money. "I spend a lot of time taking care of donors and finding new donors through contacts and corporations or getting friendly with the people as they come in as subscribers—getting them to feel the excitement and the importance of what we're doing and letting them come backstage a little to get really excited. I connect people with the company and make them know how important they are to its survival."

She responds particularly to the challenge of getting men involved. Through Edward Villella's masculine presence and Toby's ingenuity, they have overcome the traditional male reluctance to support or attend the ballet. Toby described one especially ingenious tactic she used:

One of my successes was an evening at dinner at a couple's home. She loved ballet and wanted to get her husband involved. He said he absolutely would not go to the ballet. He thought it was awful, boring, and all that. I noticed that he had a large classical music collection and asked him if he liked music. Of course, he replied, he loved music. So I said I'd make a deal with him. I'd give him tickets and he could come to the ballet and sit there with his eyes closed and just listen to the music. He thought that was very funny and said he'd come. Well, he came, and now he's chairman of the finance committee. He fell in love with it. He had no idea that this was such an exciting company—it moves with great speed and is extremely athletic and oh, so passionate!

Much of what Toby does with the ballet she does simply for the pleasure of involving young people, both as audience and as artists. The company is committed to educating young people about dance and brings in youngsters from the surrounding school districts and social service agencies, as well as Boy Scouts, Girl Scouts, and Big Brothers and Sisters, for free performances. After gaining the audience's attention with leaps, twirls, and spins, members of the young company explain the ballet. Toby says she is extremely proud of the young men and women in the company and never tires of watching them practice and perform.

Maybe I went into all of this for selfish reasons, so I could see ballet as often as I wanted. My greatest joy is when I get really tired and frustrated, I go down and watch a class. I love to watch rehearsals. It's so exciting to watch a piece start from the beginning and end up on the stage and watch how the different choreographers work. I love to watch the dancers develop from when they first come in right out of ballet school until they become soloists and principal dancers. It's very rewarding to see them express themselves at a higher professional level when they go from being dancers to real performers. You know, the exciting thing is to see young dancers get out there at a performance and finally stop dancing steps and start dancing—stop doing steps and throw themselves to the lights and become ballerinas.

Toby's passion does not include trying to run things. She has consistently turned down the position of president, not because she doubts her abilities to lead but because "I believe that the more authority and responsibility you spread out, the more likely this project will succeed." She is pleased that the board has a woman president and that both company managers are women. A little over half of the fifty-two board members are women, and she calls them a "give or get board." "It is understood when you come on the board that you have to give or raise a hundred thousand dollars every year."

A generous and friendly person, Toby seems very secure in life. Her three children are grown and love the arts, no doubt because of their early contact but also, we suspect, because Toby does not take herself or her efforts so seriously that they cannot be fun. In fact, she makes fun happen. She recounts what she did to commemorate an occasion that most women would choose to ignore—her fiftieth birthday.

> One of the most fun things I ever did in my life was when I commissioned and underwrote a ballet for my fiftieth birthday. The first year of the company, I fell in love with the work of choreographer Jimmy Gamonet De Los Heros and asked him if he would do a ballet for my birthday, at that time six years away. The contract for this ballet was for six years, and Jimmy choreographed a step a month during that time. The only thing I had was the right of refusal on the music. He was beginning to get into some contemporary music that my ears didn't want to hear over and over again. I wanted to hear my ballet. So when he was on one of his trips, he came back with Dvořák's *Serenade for Strings* and played it for me. It was magnificent. Then we had to have a name for the ballet and kept trying various versions of my maiden name, Lerner. Finally, I said, if you're going to use my name, why not use Toby? Edward [Villella] began calling it *Tobiniana*, and I loved it. So the ballet is *Tobiniana Opus 22*. I hoped that it would inspire other people to celebrate wonderful occasions in the same way, and it did. As a result of my ballet, a couple underwrote one last year for their forty-fifth anniversary because they thought it was such a fun idea.

Now that the company is firmly established, we asked her what else she wants to accomplish. Not content to be a local success,

Toby believes that with adequate funding, the Miami City Ballet can become one of the top three companies in the country, if not the world. She has utter confidence in Villella's vision for the company to become a major player, leader, and influence in the dance world. Surely her dedication and consummate ability to raise and give money, coupled with Villella's direction, will bring this about. "I view this as a lifelong dream," she insists, "and a lifelong commitment. And hopefully, in my lifetime, we'll see it with a strong enough financial endowment that we know it's going to be here long after Edward and I are gone. But it's like a child. You have a lifelong commitment to that child, although the ways you interact change over different periods."

Later on that afternoon, while watching the company putting the finishing touches on *Swan Lake*, we could not help but notice the troupe's energy and sense of fun, camaraderie, and sharing—characteristics that also describe its creator. Toby and Villella have brought together not only a ballet company but also a family of dancers who care as much about one another as they do about dance.

Kay Vaughan and Phyllis Huffman

Milwaukee, Wisconsin

Kay Vaughan and Phyllis Huffman are strong, independent women who have spent most of their lives as homemakers. However, they enjoy a sharing and equal relationship with their husbands, despite being from an age when this was not the norm.

Both are graduates of the University of Wisconsin, Madison, and strong contributors to the university. Kay provided the start-up funding for the Center for Women and Philanthropy in the School of Family Resources and Consumer Sciences (formerly the home economics program, from which Kay and Phyllis graduated). Kay's husband, Jim, was a member of the cabinet during the university's successful $435 million campaign. He retired in 1982, after which they returned to live in Milwaukee following a twenty-year absence. Both Jim and Phyllis serve on the UW Foundation Board, the fundraising arm of the university.

Phyllis and her husband, Bill, have pledged $1 million to the university and $560,000 to South Wood County 2000, a recreational and cultural project in Wisconsin Rapids, where they once lived and ran a family-owned newspaper. After the paper was sold in 1983, they moved to Milwaukee and currently divide their time between that city and New York.

We have known both women for a number of years and count them among our friends on the steering committee of the Center for Women and Philanthropy. They are equally active in the Women's Council of the Bascom Hill Society. We spoke with them prior to a Women's Council seminar in Madison.

They reminisced about what it was like at the university when they were students before and after World War II, right after the Depression. Phyllis said that she felt that being on campus following the war years provided women with unusual leadership opportunities.

Both Phyllis and Kay grew up in middle-class families in which the fathers worked for income and the mothers tended to the home and community activities. But a major difference between the families they grew up in and those they formed as adults is the relationship they enjoy with their husbands. Each woman has had a significant role in her husband's success and expected no less than a partnership position in the marriage. Kay says, "I always felt that I was partly responsible for his success and that we had an equal partnership—what we had was *ours*." That partnership extends to their giving. Although both women do most of their giving with their husbands, each expressed the freedom to support organizations of her own choice. Kay and her husband have set up an annual philanthropic budget, and the money goes to things they support individually and mutually. Outside of that budget, Kay says, "when something comes up that is of interest to me, I talk about it with Jim before committing the money, but I know he wouldn't tell me I couldn't do it."

Unlike the 1950s, when many women went to college with the primary expectation of finding a husband, the time when Kay and Phyllis went to college saw many women preparing to make a living for themselves upon graduation. Kay even put off marriage until she had proved to herself and Jim that she could get by on her own. Although she was a textiles major, she went to work for Kimberly-Clark after graduation and ended up in the personnel office. When World War II began and the men operating the heavy paper-making machinery joined the military, Kay was responsible for breaking down the barriers that kept women out of those jobs. In retrospect, Kay believes that working outside the home was one of the best decisions she has made. "It gave me the confidence to know that I could do it, and when you have the confidence and have faced corporate budgets, you know you will be able to handle babies, crises in the home, and other emergencies very capably. Women who haven't worked don't have that confidence, even though they may be very capable and even though all their volunteer work may have given them a better background than a lot of jobs do."

Phyllis also worked outside the home after graduation in a public relations position with the American Honey Institute. Following her husband's graduation in 1950, they went to Wisconsin Rapids to manage the family enterprises. Phyllis continued working for the institute as a writer until after the birth of her third child. She asserts that this experience amply provides her with her own credentials.

Volunteering has played an important role in the married lives of both women and still does for Phyllis. In New York City, she is a docent at the American Craft Museum, where she takes groups of children through the museum, explaining the exhibits. Working one on one has replaced committee activities for her because of "the satisfaction I receive from personally working with the people and seeing that I have made a difference." She reads to the visually impaired at a Lighthouse program and works in an elementary school in her neighborhood once a week with a student who has trouble reading. The written word is very important to Phyllis, who would like to have been an English major and writer. "But," she explains, "my family was very conservative and very proper. I got the definite impression that there were only two fields open to women—nursing and teaching. Home economics was one of the fields in which you could write. This was a viable thing for a young and proper woman to do." She adds laughingly, "And I was young and very proper." One has the feeling that she has expertly managed to break out of the mold cast for her by the times while still maintaining a reserved dignity of which her parents would have approved.

Kay and Phyllis have been involved in the Women's Council of the University of Wisconsin Foundation's Bascom Hill Society. They have considered the topic of women and giving for some time and participated in the Wingspread Conference on Women and Philanthropy held in October 1992.

As for the difference in the size of charitable checks written by men and by women, Kay refers to the "bake sale mentality." Many women, she says, "feel that they are doing pretty well when they get twenty-five cents for something they made, whereas a man would get on the phone and make a call asking for a hundred dollars. Women are used to looking at their household budget, while men are looking at a corporate budget where a thousand dollars is peanuts. It's that 'bake sale' mentality that women have to work to overcome."

Phyllis says that we have to get beyond the "widow's mite" to the "widow's might." "I think it's hard to get women to think larger than the small weekly donations they might give to their church. It's hard to start thinking in a bigger way." When we asked how to do this, she came forward with a wonderful idea: "One of the things that corporations can do is to solicit prospective donors among wives of CEOs, wives who have acceptance because of their husband's position and their own place in the community." Kay suggested to her husband, a member of UW's campaign cabinet and chair of the foundation, that when calls are made, husbands be asked where their wives went to school and, if it was the University of Wisconsin, whether they were supporting their program on campus.

Kay, in particular, feels that a different approach should be used with women donors, prospects, and volunteer fundraisers—an approach more aligned with their interests. She thinks that men consider the money more of a status issue—as volunteer fundraisers go to the corporate sector and try to persuade prospects to give more than a specific peer. "This doesn't work with women. You have to tell a woman what the problem is and what the solution is and how she can be a part of that. A name on a building doesn't necessarily do it either for a woman," she says.

The enthusiasm of Kay and Phyllis is crucial to the success of the University of Wisconsin Women's Council, the Center for Women and Philanthropy, and the National Network on Women as Philanthropists. These organizations would not have come into their own without the early support and interest of these two leaders, who were talking about women and giving and making their own giving decisions long before most of us were aware that we could.

Mary Gellerstedt

Atlanta, Georgia

Mary Gellerstedt needed no outside event to realize her full potential as a philanthropist. Like Phyllis and Kay, she has a supportive husband who understands and appreciates the contribution that his wife has made to his career. These men, unlike most of their generation, have encouraged an equal partnership in marriage. Similar to the riddle of the chicken and the egg, it is difficult to know which came first: the woman's independence and self-confidence or the man's support.

Mary and Lawrence Gellerstedt's families go back several generations in Atlanta history. Mary's father was chief justice of the state supreme court, and her husband has a legacy of conservative banking. Mary's mother came to terms with her own strong independent streak when she got her Realtor's license at the age of fifty. The last of her children had left home, and though she had never worked a day outside the home, she prospered in the real estate business for several years.

Before flying to Atlanta in spring 1993 for the National Society of Fundraising Executives (NSFRE) international conference, we telephoned some people there and asked what woman philanthropist they could recommend for this book. Mary's name came up time and again, as she and her husband are major supporters of nearly all of the city's cultural organizations, in particular the Atlanta Symphony and the Woodruff Art Center. Mary also serves on the board of trustees at Spelman College.

We met this gracious and soft-spoken woman in the office building of the family commercial contracting business—a business that built the Georgia Dome and is now in the process of completing the Olympic Stadium for the Games in 1996. Despite Mary's obvious ease and position in Atlanta society, she is a bit of a rebel in the causes she chooses to support. She has found the time and the money to sustain AIDS research, Planned Parenthood, and an inner-city church that the family attends, having been longstanding advocates of integration.

Another of Mary's projects is the Atlanta Women's Fund, which is part of the Metropolitan Atlanta Community Foundation. To help their fundraising efforts, Mary introduced groups of prospects to the fund by hosting a luncheon for sixty at a downtown restaurant. She believes it important for the fund to remain in the community foundation to attract the support of older women. "Women will get used to writing checks to the foundation after their husband's death. They may also feel more comfortable writing checks to the Women's Fund."

The 1992 elections were a catalyst for Mary to become involved in politics, and she helped form the Women's Political Action Committee in Atlanta. This group raised and distributed $100,000 to pro-choice female candidates in the state of Georgia, who were also supporters of women's issues. She is proud of their success in several elections and satisfied that they received a great deal of public notice in many others. She feels that because of the attention, more voters will consider these candidates in future elections.

Although this book is about women, in Mary Gellerstedt's case it is difficult not to include her husband, as he has played such an important part in her philanthropy. We were impressed by both her self-confidence and his support. Their alma maters receive equal amounts—definitely not the case in most families. And as the family business has grown and their giving has increased, their children have received the benefit of learning about philanthropy from both parents equally. "We taught the children about giving as they grew up," Mary explains, "and always felt that it was important that all of us be involved in the giving process. We have a saying in our family—'You have to pay your civic rent,' meaning that you should actually be working in the community to do things, since we're not here for free. That is something that our children are following along with."

Mary is well aware of the differences between women's giving and men's, particularly in the South. Alicia Philipp, executive director of the Metropolitan Atlanta Community Foundation, has said, "Women in the South haven't taken control of their money. There are women who give but not as much as their husbands give." Mary had this to add:

Many women give out of their grocery money and need to learn to give from their assets. Men think in terms of larger gifts, but the fact is that women live longer and are the final arbiters of the family's wealth. Because they haven't been given the responsibility of handling money or financial statements, they are often afraid to ask for them, not wanting a confrontation. Women are the peacemakers in the family and feel a responsibility to keep everything and everyone congenial. We need to provide women with a comfort level about their money so that they will give more, and I'm thrilled to say that I am seeing greater interest on women's part in learning about finance. We are putting on planned-giving seminars at the Woodruff Art Center, and more older women are coming to these than I have seen before.

Unlike many of her contemporaries, Mary has not been afraid to ask for money or take positions of leadership in the city. No doubt she has been invited to serve because of her self-confidence, philanthropic leadership, and convictions, which she is not afraid to express. This has been an asset for the organizations she supports but sometimes causes ripples in the social circles in which she and her husband travel. One tale, told in her soft southern voice, went like this: "We were at a dinner party, and a discussion about Clarence Thomas arose. I realized that the concept of sexual harassment held by the others at the table was very old-fashioned and began to enlighten them. When I really got into the subject, I could feel Lawrence kicking me repeatedly under the table. I finally said, 'I know you're kicking me, and I know you want me to hush, but I'm not going to until I finish!'"

Despite such little skirmishes, Mary says, she enjoys a marriage marked by mutual respect, openness, and a sense of humor. "I'm married to someone who thinks you should be assertive. He has always encouraged me to be myself and to think for myself."

One of her most delightful stories is about the time she and Lawrence cochaired a $35 million capital campaign at her alma mater, Agnes Scott. Their leadership positions caused an interesting confrontation. "As open as Lawrence is with his concepts of women, in the first three or four weeks he chaired the meetings, he kept asking me to carry out things that needed to be done. Finally, I stopped by his office one day and said that I was going to resign because I wasn't used to being a secretary when I had been appointed a cochair. He just roared with laughter. He hadn't even realized what he was doing. We still laugh about it today."

The story has a happy ending as Mary and Lawrence met their campaign goal together as a team—an ending that is in harmony with their marriage. According to Mary, "Everything we have done has been as a team. We were always there to back one another up in the business, with the children, and socially. Our best buddy has always been each other."

This elegant and charming woman is proud of the strides she has made in her personal life and the differences she has brought about through her public involvement. She is also very clear about the difference between giving time and giving money. "The whole thing isn't volunteering. I didn't want to be just an envelope stuffer; I wanted to be involved. Like with the abortion issue: I wanted to make a change. I wanted to give not only my time but also my money and my effort to make a change. I could do that because I've had a good life. The more I've been exposed to, the more interested I have become in making more changes. And it's been fun too. The end result is that I was there, I was involved, and I made a difference."

Rose Johnson

Evanston, Illinois

When we interviewed Rose Johnson, she was grieving over a close friend whom she had just learned was dying. Rose had seen her three months earlier, looking healthy and robust, during a visit to Chicago. This tragedy seemed to make Rose, at fifty-six, sensitive to her own mortality and stronger in her commitment to helping others. "Deep down inside, I'm looking for the ability to ease the path of young black women who are walking in the same shoes I walked in forty years ago. Although their obstacles are even greater than mine were, to be able to facilitate someone else's way is my ambition. So many people were helpful in making my way."

Rose was born in Tallahassee, Florida, to parents who both had some college education. Her father and mother were divorced when she was thirteen. Her mother did domestic work because, as Rose explained, in those days it was very difficult for black people to get jobs other than in factories or as household employees. The family's income was very meager, and although she was an only child, Rose doubts whether she would have been able to attend college had it not been for the United Negro College Fund. She was awarded a scholarship to Spelman College in Atlanta, Georgia. She recalls, "In 1953, I had just enough money for the train fare to Atlanta. My aunt and uncle let me live with them my first year, and from then on, I worked on campus, making thirty cents an hour doing office work. But a summer job and my mother's help enabled me to live in a dorm during my last three years."

Rose's years at Spelman provided inspiration for a lifetime. Although not an especially religious person, she fondly recalls the daily chapel and frequent speeches of distinguished guests, such as Rev. Howard Thurman, a Morehouse graduate; Dr. Samuel Du Bois Cook, now president of Dillard University, in New Orleans; Whitney Young, who was then a professor at Atlanta University; and Mattiwilda Dobbs, a Spelman graduate and world-renowned soprano. "These special people spoke to all of us from the podium. Their message, over and over, was that when we finished our studies, we weren't through; we had a responsibility to the community at large to contribute not only money but also services to the less fortunate. We owed something for the privilege of attending Spelman. I took this advice very seriously."

In comparing her education with that of her friends and her

husband, who graduated from Roosevelt University in Chicago, Rose notes that many black students experienced a lack of support during the transition from high school to college at larger, predominantly white institutions, in many cases leading to the students' flunking out. "Spelman's atmosphere was one of nurturing. People who were not necessarily great scholars were provided with opportunities and nurtured to become some of the best performers in their fields, as well as contributing members of society," she says.

As might be expected, Rose is a strong financial supporter and volunteer for her alma mater, giving generous annual donations. Spelman is currently involved in phase two of its capital campaign to raise $80 million. Rose acknowledged that the campaign has not been an easy task due mainly to the still comparatively limited financial means of most Spelman graduates. According to the college's vice president for institutional advancement, Billie Sue Schulze, generous gifts of $20 million from Camille and Bill Cosby and $37 million from the DeWitt Wallace/Spelman College fund in the New York Community Trust form the nucleus of the funds raised so far. Phase two, in benefit of the sciences and certain high-priority renovation projects, will focus on corporate gifts while also reaching out to trustees, friends, and alumni for assistance in planning and solicitation, in addition to a new level of financial commitment.

Through the empowerment fostered by the Cosby and Wallace gifts, the college plans to enhance and build a comprehensive fundraising program with graduates like Rose Johnson. Working closely with Wellesley College, of which Rose's elder daughter is a graduate, Spelman modified its successful campaign and is "taking the show on the road to twenty different cities over a three-year period," according to Schulze. It was at one of these events in Chicago that we first met Rose. A dinner for Chicago-area alumnae at the headquarters of the historic black sorority Alpha Kappa Alpha was followed by a focus group and rating session with fifty women present. The gathering included both graduates and parents of current students.

During the evening's activities, Rose's leadership was outstanding. The focus group was very informal and deliberately conducted like a debriefing session, where people could talk about their Spelman years, alumnae news, and what programs should be part of the curriculum. Her recent experience as an Evanston school board member was evident, as time and again she spoke up and helped facilitate the discussion and consolidate opinions.

When we asked why she decided to give up her teaching career to run for the school board, she pointed out the conflict of interest in acting as her own employer. But, she said, the major motivator was a strong belief in education. "I really do believe in the power of education and the fact that every child is educable. Education is the key to lifelong success for all children. In fact, I get very emotional about this and have broken down and cried at meetings a few times, talking about the plight of black children today."

Rose is very proud of the cooperative spirit on the board of seven, four of whom are women. "We have a very compatible board," she observes, "although we're not always completely in lockstep. One of the impressive things that I have seen happen over the past two years is our increased ability to listen to one another and understand that one person alone isn't capable of making decisions—that three others are needed to bring an issue to closure."

Rose strongly believes in training women to become leaders and feels that Spelman provided her with that opportunity. She, in turn, is a member and supporter of Leadership Illinois, an offshoot of Leadership America. This networking organization helps its members, corporate and managerial women, learn firsthand lobbying techniques for making changes in government. Members also organize informal reunions to talk about major issues facing the state and the nation.

In discussing her community fundraising efforts, Rose makes an energetic case for women to get themselves on boards where their influence can be used to leverage money for causes they consider important. She recounted a Kiwanis meeting she attended earlier that morning: "We have grants to seven organizations, four of which are ones I've been associated with. My influence in Kiwanis is due to having worked with several organizations and having introduced fellow Kiwanians to them and their good works."

An understanding, supportive, and generous husband has been a great help to Rose throughout their marriage of thirty-two years. Bob Johnson climbed the corporate ladder to become vice president of Sears before he left to begin a business in Memphis with their elder daughter. According to Rose, her husband has become more sensitive and less chauvinistic over the years. "Maybe that's because of living with three strong women," she suggests. (Their younger daughter is a wildlife ecologist for the state of Missouri.) "We have always considered that all the money was ours, which worked very well for me because when we were both making the same amount, we put it into the pot and had equal access to it. Then when he started moving up, it remained the same, so I have always had the same amount of control over the money. We give the same amounts to our colleges, and he feels as strongly about Spelman as I do."

Rose attributes much of her sense of community responsibility to her mother, who two decades ago took care of Rose's young daughter on the South Side of Chicago while Rose taught school. "Mama has always cared for children, and she is the one who showed me how to give and share with others. I can't say enough about my two mothers: Spelman and my real mother. They have had the greatest influence on what I am and what I do," she says.

Conclusion

So there you are, eight different women, eight different stories, and many common threads. Maddie, Harriet, and Jo were strongly influenced in their philanthropy by members of their families of origin. For Phyllis, Kay, Mary, and Rose, it was their husbands and their full-partnership marriages that provided the encouragement and inspiration to help them realize their potential as philanthropists.

The eight women have different expectations about women's giving and asking others for gifts. Maddie and Toby were the most optimistic about the ability of women to ask for money; the others saw women as needing a great deal of education before taking their rightful place.

Creating something that they cared deeply, even passionately about was an experience shared by Harriet, Jo, Toby, and Maddie. Each woman had, through her efforts and gifts, given birth to projects with which she remains heavily involved and committed to. The Old Main renovation for Maddie, the Miami City Ballet for Toby, and women's funds for Harriet and Jo were actually philanthropic conduits through which these women were able to express their entrepreneurial spirit.

These women have enormous self-confidence, which, combined with their wealth and access, makes them powerful forces in their communities and causes. Relaxed and knowledgeable about their money and aware of how it can be used to leverage change, they have grown to the point where giving money is great personal fun.

All of the women have at some point been professional volunteers, and most continue in that capacity. But they fully understand the financial commitment that goes along with volunteerism and the opportunities they have to bring about change through their leadership in the nonprofit sector.

Each woman has created something unique to her individual needs and lifestyle. Each has found a way to integrate her values into her philanthropy. Each is giving money, doing good, and having fun. We are in awe of their confidence and their sense of inner power and competence. Women like these are the role models for a whole new generation of good works.

Part Two

Cultivating Women Donors

Chapter Four

How and Why Women Give

Women are bringing an original and discriminating voice to philanthropy, a voice that differs markedly from that of their male counterparts. Women's giving preferences reflect their upbringing and lifelong societal conditioning. Women's philanthropic motivations, or values, are a product of socialization and a collective feminine history that is vastly divergent from that of males. Rather than focus on biological or physiological explorations, we have chosen to listen to what women tell us about giving—what motivates them to give and why.

We have conducted personal interviews, focus groups, and discussions with scores of women philanthropists throughout the United States. Their responses reveal that women are breaking out of the "passive woman philanthropist" mold that resulted in their seeking anonymity as donors or the Lady Bountiful image in the public view. We asked women what being a philanthropist means to them and what they personally gain from their philanthropy.

What Does It Mean to Be a Philanthropist?

The dictionary defines *philanthropy* as "love and goodwill toward all people." We thought that it would be interesting to uncover a working definition of philanthropy from a female perspective. Women in our focus groups and interviews live up to the dictionary definition, caring deeply about making the world a better place through their philanthropy. Their experiences, perspectives, and intent are clearly reflected in their own words:

> "I think in terms of incremental improvement in the world and the community when I'm gone, So that when I die, I will have put a little more back into it than I took out."

> "To me philanthropy means being able to show love for humankind and goodwill to all people."

> "I think it's a general attitude you have toward everything you contact and you get in touch with. You have a friendly feel for it and listen to it and help in any way you can."

> "Philanthropy is a feeling of sharing and of supporting things you know to have a need. It's also a feeling of empowering others, giving back to the world, and something you should do."

> "Philanthropy is sharing your good fortune. It's a sense of having so much when there are so many needs."

Women are aware that in today's world, this mission must be translated into a responsibility to give money: "I feel a sense of humility—that I don't deserve what I have any more than the next person. But everyone deserves a good life, and there's enough to go around in this country. I think with women, too often that humility is not paired with the value of what we're giving. We don't feel enough custodianship over the dollars that we may be giving. I think in a lot of women, the humility is there or the sense of obligation, but then you also have to have the sense of responsibility to take care of it."

There is also a holistic aspect to their definition of philanthropy. The world would be a better place not only for others but also for them: "I guess I would define it in two ways. One is sharing your good fortune. But I also see it in another way: acting in your own self-interests—if my neighbor is OK, my life is going to be OK even more."

Passing on the responsibility of philanthropy to their children is of great importance to many of these women. They related philanthropy to their children in different ways, and even women without children thought about it in terms of giving to the future:

"To me it also means giving back to this world and really giving from my heart. Giving to what is meaningful that reflects my values. It is also the responsibility I have as a parent to teach things to my children to help them think about giving to their community and to this society."

"I don't have children, so in philanthropy I'm looking for a way to give something to the future the way parents give through their children."

"Now that I have children, I'm very aware of a sense of belonging that I never felt before, belonging to a community. Now I have a sense of responsibility to something. I need to give back, and I need to instruct my children."

Not everyone understands that a philanthropist does not have to be a Rockefeller or a Ford. However, all understand the value of combining forces and money for the common good: "The idea that you don't have to be a member of a family with a great fortune to be a philanthropist has particular appeal. It makes you think about the strength of numbers that may be able to accomplish something. And that you, as an individual of more limited means, can have an impact on the larger issues."

Given the success of political fundraising for female candidates in 1992, we were curious about whether women regarded political contributions as philanthropy. The responses indicate that they do not consider it pure philanthropy because of a measure of self-interest involved. Many women acknowledged that they had not been particularly involved in politics before 1992 and still thought it somewhat impure. But they are realistic enough to know that to bring about change, it is necessary to elect people who share their values and political beliefs:

> "I don't think politics is as altruistic as other fields—there's an element of self-interest there."

> "I consider political action a kind of social responsibility, something that I do not just for myself but because I care about other people."

> "I gave more last year because of my concerns about what is happening. Since I took away from other charitable causes, I guess I would consider it philanthropic."

Clearly, women prefer to think of their philanthropy as selfless and involving a high measure of fellowship, obligation, and the ability to make a difference.

Philanthropic Rewards

We were curious about what personal reward women get from their philanthropy. Again, their responses indicate altruism accompanied by a sense of self-empowerment and the reward of feeling part of a larger community—an association that can improve the present and influence the future: "By giving to an organization I support, I am also empowering myself to be a part of that organization and carry on its value system."

Friendships that arise from philanthropic involvement are another dividend for many women, be it the joy of meeting others who share their interests and values or the opportunity to meet people that they would not be likely to meet otherwise: "My involvement as a donor is tied up with the fact that I get to be with just absolutely wonderful women and men who share the same passions as I do about making the world a better place for women and girls."

Other rewards include being a part of a process and holding a privileged position from which to watch a project unfold: "One of the rewards for me is being around the creative process of really top-notch creative people. Such involvement is very rare for people who are not among the founders."

We asked the women if they had considered the potential for leveraging their gift. Most had not, and many were repelled by the notion. They did not view their philanthropy as a play for power or position and consequently had not thought about the results that they could achieve by making their gifts conditional on specific organizational or policy changes:

"I think it happens the other way round. You get involved, and you feel you owe something, and then you give."

"I don't give to become a leader in an organization. That's what men do, and I don't see a value in that."

"I think we see that attitude dominating corporate philan-thropy—self-interest. We shouldn't be applying that to ourselves."

Others feel that it would not make any difference if a woman gave a large gift because her husband would be credited with it any-way: "Men make large donations and are pulled into the leadership. Women make large donations, and it is assumed it came from their husbands. Maybe it's not a realistic expectation that women will be pulled into leadership through their contributions."

An African-American woman expressed a similar pattern in her community, where "people who give often are the leaders. That is part of our culture." But when asked if it was gender-related, she laughed and said, "Like others, we have a chauvinis-tic culture."

Motivations: The Six C's of Women's Giving

Harold J. Seymour (1988) devotes the first chapter of *Designs for Fundraising*, the fundraiser's bible, to a discussion of "universal motivations" that lead to popular funding support for programs. However, Seymour's "universal" motivations apply almost entirely to men. His theories are not across-the-board truisms; as we discovered in our interviews and discussions, women's motivations are quite different from those of men.

If there are any universals in what motivates women to give, they can be summed up in six categories, all beginning with the letter C: the desire to change, create, connect, commit, collaborate, and celebrate their philanthropic accomplishments.

Change

The ability to bring about change and make a difference ranks number one as a motivation for women's giving. Women are willing to support new and different causes and prefer to give where their gift will make a difference. For women, making a difference means making a change, rather than preserving the status quo. They think of themselves as the agents of this change:

"I have developed myself into a tool for change."

"I want to effect change. I want to give not only my time but also my money and my efforts to make a change. The more I've been exposed to, the more interested I have become in making more changes."

Women's motivations for change can be compared with their political interests. Studies indicate that women run for office and support political candidates out of a desire to see a justice served, to address a need, or to make a difference (Sublett and Stone, 1993, pp. 4–6). The 1992 elections provided them with the expectation of changing the system: "All the people giving are doing so for social change. They are giving money where permanent change can take place—not for the candidate but for the cause."

Many women have felt the sting of inequality and prejudice. Because of this, they want to make things better, not only for the less fortunate but also for the girls and young women coming up behind them. They do not want their daughters to have to go through the difficulties and struggles that they did: "I think there is a ton of injustice. I'm interested not only in correcting that but also in making other people aware of it."

Women see money as a tool for change, and they see change as immediate, not gradual, as revolutionary, not reformed. Women want to see their money have a visible effect. Many women, in fact, find it difficult to support large, mainstream agencies because of the typical bureaucratic structure that inhibits change: "I will give to people who will make a change rather than an agency. Women want to create change and be a part of the organization in the community. They can't do that through agencies."

Some women are savvy enough to understand the importance of targeting their money to maximize their clout:

"I would rather give more money to one cause and make a difference than take that same amount of money and spread it around."

"The end result is that I was there, I was involved, and I made a difference."

Create

For many women, giving to change the status quo means helping create a new order. This entrepreneurial desire to create may explain the growth and popularity of women's funds over the past decade. These funds are a way for women to originate something concrete and at the same time deal with issues affecting women and children: "Women have a predisposition to make connections in a humane way that can live on after their lives are over. If they are allowed involvement in the creative process of developing philanthropic innovations, not Band-Aid solutions, they are very likely to create things that will live on far beyond their lifetimes."

Certainly this was true of the women philanthropists in the nineteenth and early twentieth centuries. Many of the institutions they created have lived on well beyond the donor's lifetime and are still providing education, culture, and services for the needy. Because this kind of philanthropy is a creation akin to birth, many women regard their projects as they would their children: "A cause is like a child, and you have a lifelong commitment and responsibility to that child."

As with all new life, the birthing process can take a long time and is often frustrating. Fundraisers may need patience and diligence in working with female prospects. It is not easy getting women together to do something unfamiliar. Not only do most women not consider themselves philanthropists, but they are not familiar with leadership positions to the extent that men are. Many women are unaware of how an organization operates or how to set one up.

But women's energy, enthusiasm, and intelligence make up for the lengthy work sessions and trial-and-error tinkering. Most rewarding is their dedication as they move through the process. When a man gives money, that is usually the end of the negotiations. The reverse is true with a woman: by giving money, she is beginning a long-term relationship with the organization.

Connect

Women want to feel connected with an organization when they give money. Fundraisers can encourage this sense of connection in a number of ways, starting before approaching a female prospect for money and continuing beyond the receipt of the gift.

The first kind of connection should begin well in advance of asking for a gift. By connecting women with our organization or project before asking them for money, we let our prospects know that we care about them.

For example, when one major university tried to solicit women prospects, it learned that they felt no connection whatsoever with the institution. This discovery led the development staff to initiate a program to attract more women donors—a situation in which everyone wins. The university wins because it enlarges its prospect pool, and the women win because they have the opportunity to discuss what appeals to them and what they are interested in supporting.

Another organization thought it had just the program women would support—a women's history project that included funding for a video of a women's history conference. A development officer solicited her women board members following a meeting and, to her dismay, met with extreme hostility. The board members had not been informed of the project during its two-year existence and had a great many questions regarding it. No early connection had been established, and the women were insulted at being asked to become involved at such a late date, particularly when the assumption was made that they would be interested solely because the project concerned women.

Two good lessons can be learned from this example: do not assume that women are interested in a project simply because it is about women, and give them an opportunity to connect and create, if possible from the beginning. Attempting to involve women later rarely succeeds.

The second type of connection is linking the organization or cause with something meaningful to the woman. "Women want to be part of an organization. We need to cultivate and then connect women to the organization," said one female donor.

. This can often add considerably to the time required to procure a woman's gift. However, without the effort, you risk getting a reduced gift or none at all. Alicia Philipp, executive director of the Metropolitan Atlanta Community Foundation, has this to say about connecting women to the cause: "It takes a lot more nurturing to get gifts from women. It's a long-term process. With men, you get an answer after making the pitch. With women, it's a cultivating process. They need to think about it, and it takes more than one visit, involving multiple calls and writing notes to follow up. Women want to touch, see, and feel. They want to know who else is giving. With men, it's positioning among their peers."

Women can be brought into the group through current or potential friendships with others who are involved.

A large part of linking women to an organization involves making them feel needed. To some degree, everyone wants to be needed, but women have been ignored in the philanthropic area for so long that it is particularly important to them. And there are distinct benefits to be derived from attending to their needs:

"If women feel needed by an institution, a wonderful, maternal syndrome is set in motion; they begin to regard the institution as they would a child. They want to talk about it, to see that its special needs are met, that it is introduced to the right people."

"I don't feel hesitant about calling on women for money because they want to be connected with the organization and recognized as needed."

Perhaps the most important connection the organization can offer its female donors is a continuing link following the gift. This can be as simple as a thank-you: "So often I give a contribution and there is no follow-up to the gift, no thank-you. I see [the recipients] on the street, and they don't even recognize me. But sure enough, when the next solicitation sweep comes around, I'm on their list."

Most women donors also appreciate newsletters and reports

updating them on the project they have funded. Personal visits are especially welcome, particularly if the donor can meet a recipient of the fund program, such as a student on a scholarship: "I prefer my continuing contact to be further away from the development office—someone from the project or the cause."

Many women consider this kind of connection the most important and worthwhile recognition they receive, and it may be needed to ensure future gifts: "We gave a chair to [an eastern university]. If they don't keep in touch, we won't give again or put them in our will. Actually, that makes it easier, because our giving means more to others that do keep in touch."

As we begin to establish connections in the field of women and philanthropy, it will be interesting to note whether the time involved in obtaining women's gifts decreases. We suspect that it will.

Commit

Women are committed to giving, although their expression of this commitment has traditionally been through volunteer work. Even as their lives have become busier, women remain committed to volunteerism. This can be problematic for development officers who wish to convince their female prospects that organizations and institutions need not only their hours but also their dollars to be able to continue. However, with planning, fundraisers can use this commitment to volunteerism to get women to help procure major gifts. In the words of one woman philanthropist: "We must find a new way of attracting women to charities by using their strong volunteer orientation yet focusing on major giving. The dollars speak the loudest. We must educate women about the process."

Many women volunteer for an organization before giving money, but many committed volunteers are never asked or even expected to contribute. This neglect is a loss for both the women and the organization:

"I've been involved with the Girl Scouts for a long time. I've given time but never money, and we're always trying to figure out how to raise money. My husband's involved with the Boy Scouts, and he gets all his friends together for a $200 breakfast, and they have their fundraising done like that."

"I worked at a day-care center when my children were smaller. The center asked me to volunteer two hours a week, and it was hard to quantify the value of what I did. But the point is, no one ever asked me for money, too."

There are still women who believe that if they volunteer, they will be excused from the obligation to give money. Some, in fact, expect strong recognition for their volunteer time. Fortunately, that attitude is declining, and others know that being on a board means being expected to give: "I sit on a utility board, and the shareholders look at you and say, 'If you're not buying into this company, why should I support it?' The same analogy holds true for nonprofits. If I do not invest in this organization myself, how can I ask foundations, corporations, and other individuals to do so?"

Historically, women have given generously of their time because that was all they had to give. But as more women take jobs outside the home and free time diminishes, many are relieved (though often unnecessarily guilt-ridden) to be able to give money rather than time. Volunteer work, meanwhile, is taking on a new dignity in society. The whole concept of service is being regarded more highly, and the volunteers themselves are taking a more professional approach to what they do.

As development officers seeking to move women beyond volunteering, we should regard them not as "little helpers" but as professionals who deserve to know how much their efforts count. This raises their self-esteem, their sense of connection to the institution, and their philanthropic sights. They will be more likely to rise to the occasion when we ask them for money.

Collaborate

To juggle the complex roles of wife, mother, daughter, and worker, women have to be able to negotiate, mediate, and adapt. Traditionally, it has been a woman's job to maintain harmony and cooperation in families and communities. Consequently, women should be in a unique position to understand the necessity and economic advantages of developing unity and working with others to solve problems. Collaboration was a key element recently in the fantastically successful capital campaign for Wellesley College. According to campaign cochair Nicki Tanner (1992, p. 3), "We spoke in many voices. The earliest voice was collaborative. We created partnerships with the alumnae even before the campaign was official. . . . We collaborated on fundraising techniques. . . . We collaborated on celebrations."

As we look at our organizations and institutions, we need to be aware of where we can work with other groups or programs within our organization to create partnerships and connect women with one another, thereby avoiding duplication, competition, and wasteful use of resources.

Celebrate

Over and over, we hear women say that they do not like asking for money. The reasons for this vary, ranging from the personal ("I don't handle rejection well") to the polite ("I don't like to put people in an awkward position"). One way to overcome this resistance is to make giving money fun, so that both asking and contributing can become more than an obligation or a responsibility.

Tracy Gary, director of Resourceful Women, an organization that helps women of wealth manage their resources and their philanthropy, recognized this and is spearheading a project called Fun Philanthropy—making giving fun. For example, one woman initiated a "birthday project" for her fiftieth birthday. Phoebe Valentine gave $10,000 each to five carefully selected friends and asked them to give the money to community agencies they believed in. After a three-month period in which the women did research and recommended where the money should go, she brought them together to talk about that experience. This was a form of celebration—women talking about what they did and why.

Even though we cannot always find women like Phoebe Valentine, we can get our own women donors together in a celebration to encourage them to talk about how much fun it is to give money and solicit ideas about their favorite projects or donations. One woman relates her story: "I was with the executive director of a folk museum. He was just panting over a certain bowl. And I thought, this is ridiculous; I can afford to buy that bowl, and I know it is going to a good cause. As a result, everyone was happy, and I knew that the bowl was going to the right home. I drove home feeling wonderful. I like to have opportunities like this periodically to give just because it feels great."

We can make giving fun through celebrations. Campaign kick-offs can be causes for celebration, and landmarks along the way can also be celebrated. The Wellesley campaign was built around celebrations, and its spectacular success speaks for this approach. Not only that, but the celebratory aspect can make fundraising more fun for development officers as well.

Deliberation and Accountability

It is not enough to appeal to women's emotions. Women also want facts before they will give. They want to know the broad rationale for the program and how the organization will carry it out. They want to know that the program is fiscally sound and capably administered. Only then can they be sure that their money will be used wisely. To explain this insistence on facts and particulars, Ruth Sweet, a communication consultant from Nashville, says, "Women are process-oriented. They want to know all the pieces in between, and they want logistics for the strategy. They're interested in details, and they want to know whom, not what, their gift affects."

One of the issues that women find disquieting are high administrative salaries and overheads, particularly in large organizations: "I try to look at how an organization is structured and how it operates. Then I try to estimate whether the dollars are actually benefiting people or whether they're supporting a big organization."

Women tend to take their giving very seriously and are concerned when charitable dollars leave their community. Many prefer giving locally because they can see results: "I think the whole United Way thing does help focus you to the local environment because you know the organizations—you know those dollars are going to go to the cause that you want to help out."

Women's preference for community extends to grassroots organizational support and targeted giving. In every instance, women can see what is happening to their money and hence feel that they can make more of a difference: "I give to small organizations where I can make a difference—minority groups and rural areas where people don't have access to services."

Many women look at their giving as an investment and feel that they are in a way purchasing stock in the organization. As when purchasing equities, bonds, or mutual funds, they want to see results. They want to know that the organization will use their money well.

As women gain positions of power and wealth, investment firms are taking a second look at how they invest. Because women themselves have made a connection between investing in the financial market and giving to nonprofits, it is worth noting what investment analysts have discovered about women investors.

In an article in the January 1992 issue of *Working Woman*, Mary Rowland cites research that concludes, "Women tend to be more careful than men with their investible cash, often shopping around before parting with it. . . . They also tend to invest with their conscience, avoiding companies that manufacture socially objectionable products or pollute the environment" (pp. 57, 59).

The article goes on to say that males generally make decisions about their investments right away, whereas most women want to think about it first and get back to the investment counselor. Also, women like to do more research on their investment than men but take a longer view of the investment, accepting slow and steady growth.

There are strong messages for development officers in these statements. If we accept the idea that women feel that they are investing in nonprofits as they invest in securities and other financial markets, we can make the following assumptions:

- Women will take longer to decide to give a gift than men.
- Women want to research the organization thoroughly before committing to making a gift.
- Once they become committed, women will stick with their decision to support the organization, even when it does not produce immediate results.
- Women are more likely to support a cause that helps others or will help make the world a better place.

Helping Others

Women have traditionally been the caregivers and the ones who hold the family together. Most female donors extend this sense of responsibility to the greater community. They see a need—a problem that leads to suffering or underachievement for an individual or a segment of the community—and want to use their gifts to solve it. As one female philanthropist explains, "I feel a responsibility to young people and families, and I will give because it touches my heart. I want my dollars to go to the families I see suffering."

Part of caring from the heart involves responding to one of the most tragic and threatening issues in America today, the AIDS crisis: "My husband and I are supporters of the AIDS Foundation. We have a best-friend couple, two gay men. We were just at an AIDS benefit last spring, and twelve of the people at the two tables of fifteen not only were HIV-positive but have AIDS. Wonderful, strapping men who are in the prime of their lives and careers, very successful men, at thirty-seven, are dying. In the next five years, we will be the only friends these two guys have left who have known them from their youth."

It may be that women address these issues because they want a better world in which to raise their children. Indeed, our research with women donors indicates that children far outrank other interest areas. In a survey of its contributors, A Fund for Women in Madison found that children ranked highest in both interest and support levels. In other words, not only are women concerned about children, but they also support programs dealing with children. However, their support level was found to be considerably below their interest level in all other areas, indicating that either they are not being asked to give at their interest level or they are not being asked in the right way. This phenomenon was true for every interest category in the survey except children (see Chapter Eleven).

By presenting female prospects with the needs of an institution in ways that are meaningful to them and challenging them to help advance its mission, development officers can help women make the transition from volunteerism to financial giving. They can begin to close the gap between women's interests and their support levels.

Women's Concerns, Influence, and Philanthropy

Incredible energy and attention surround the topic of women and philanthropy. This expanding interest and women's growing influence are being driven by women's changing economic and political status, as well as by a growing recognition that women's issues are societal issues. Jane Donowitz, who heads the Women's Campaign Fund, asserted after the 1992 elections, "It is as if some of our experiences have finally been given recognition. . . . Women may be different in terms of party and perspective, but all are interested in health care, job training, small business, the way the economy affects women" (Groer, 1993, p. 148).

An interesting and daring ad campaign was conceived before the 1992 elections by fifty women from advertising, news, and entertainment organizations, specifically targeting women and urging them to vote. The themes chosen to stimulate women to express themselves at the polls were the ones that women have been shown to care about—health care, poverty, education, and unemployment. Jeanne Chinard, executive vice president and senior creative director at the Young and Rubicam advertising agency in New York City, came up with the idea. Chinard says, "There are so many women who don't feel that they have any influence or effect on the world around them or on their own lives or on their children's lives. But in fact, they have tremendous power if they only use it" ("New Group Urges Vote . . . ," 1992).

Given women's explicitly defined concerns and vision, never before has there been such a need for their presence in the philanthropic world. The challenge and opportunity for fundraisers is to show that our institutions can meet women's vision and special interests and consequently deserve their philanthropy. In the long run, increased funding for so-called women's issues will benefit the political and economic future of the entire country. For example, day care affects the labor supply; health care, the rising national debt. Kathleen Brown, treasurer of the state of California, expressed it well at the 1992 Democratic convention when she said, "The issues that have been our issues—these are America's issues."

Reviewing women's motivations for giving, we see that by helping them establish their priorities and create and nurture programs that serve those priorities, we are assisting them in carrying out their philanthropic intent through their considerable means.

Chapter Five

Overcoming Barriers to Women's Giving

Keller Cushing Freeman, of Greenville, South Carolina, says, "Over these past thirty-seven years, I have had occasion to reflect on the conflicted nature of my relationship to money, marriage, and potential recipients of my philanthropic gratitude. My husband and I approach our giving quite differently. I will hazard a generalization that our differences run deeper than personal idiosyncrasies—they run, in fact, to the depths of gender"(personal communication).

She goes on to assert that women and men relate differently to wealth and its distribution. Women have traditionally given generously of their time and energy to causes and institutions beyond the circle of the family. As for "fiscal generosity," however, she notes that women have historically been held back because most have had little control over their finances, and to this day they earn only 70 cents to the dollar earned by men. "But in addition to the external forces of unequal pay, unequal career opportunities, and unequal control of the wealth, I strongly suspect that there have been and continue to be powerful internal hindrances to women's development of mature philanthropic attitudes," she says.

There are a number of barriers to women's giving. Some are internal characteristics of the women themselves and are often the result of socialization in a male-dominated order. Others are simply myths about women held by fundraisers. We will first discuss several myths and then examine some better-substantiated barriers to women's giving.

Myths

While many of these myths, or assumptions, contain an element of truth, they lead to an unfortunate typecasting of women as donors. As with all stereotypes, they can become self-fulfilling prophesies. It is up to development officers to identify and disregard the myths and learn to work with the characteristics of women philanthropists that have been supported with research.

1. *Women give less than men.* Studies have found that women give only 1.8 percent of their income to charity, compared with 3.1 percent for men. But it is important to consider how these figures are derived. Are we sure that women's gifts are being credited and counted fairly? Are women being asked to give at the same rate as men? The two most frequent complaints expressed in focus groups and interviews are that women's gifts have been credited to their husbands, and that women are not being asked to give at the same rate as men.

As we have seen in earlier chapters, women *are* beginning to give more. They are giving to women's funds, women's colleges, and political candidates who address the issues they care about. Women give when asked in the right way to support causes they believe in.

2. *Women give only to causes that their husbands have supported.* This often describes women who have inherited money from their husbands or fathers and feel that they should continue to donate to the institutions that these male family members supported. Fundraisers can help women identify their own values and build their philanthropic self-confidence before they inherit money by including wives and daughters in their calls when they solicit gifts from men.

3. *Male financial advisers make all the decisions for the disposition of a woman's money.* Too frequently, women of wealth defer all charitable giving to financial advisers, most of whom are men. In many

cases, this is a continuation of a woman's feeling that men were predestined to care for her. The sad consequence, however, is that her money usually goes to causes representing values other than her own.

Some financial advisers actually encourage their clients, male or female, to keep their assets high so that the advisers can make more money. Again, early education can help. Once empowered by her money, a woman will ultimately be able to deal with her financial adviser and direct her own giving.

4. *Women do not understand money or want to discuss it.* Many women consider money to be a vulgar topic of conversation. Very often their reticence to discuss financial matters is simply a ruse to avoid exposing their ignorance. However, a significant event in their lives, such as a divorce, the death of a loved one, or even a special cause that touches them deeply, can alter all of that. Time and again we have seen women take control of their money and become significant philanthropists in their own right, especially following a divorce. Previously uncomfortable discussing money, they grow to accept and even relish their philanthropic power as a new-found instrument to carry their voice.

5. *Women will give only from their disposable income.* Fundraisers who have taken the time to educate women regarding what they can accomplish with a major gift have been successful in convincing their female donors that they can take a risk and give from their assets. When Congresswoman Patricia Schroeder of Colorado asked women at fundraising luncheons around the country to "contribute at least as much as you spent on your last outfit" (Jones, 1992b, p. 8), she was educating the women about giving. She astutely used a familiar cue (the cost of a suit of clothes) plus a sprinkling of guilt.

6. *Women volunteer their time but not their money.* Understanding the difference between volunteering and philanthropy may be a difficult concept for many women, who still believe that raising

money means working hard to make something, such as a pie or a quilt, and then selling it. (This is known as the "bake sale mentality.") The actual money that goes toward the cause is not as important to these women as the effort.

Again, by taking the time to educate women about your institution's needs, you can help them see the bigger picture and their potential role as major players.

7. *If women give a large amount of money to an organization, they will want to run it.* This stereotype may fit a woman who has initiated a charity herself. Because of her daily presence, her demands on staff, and her insistence on doing things her way, the organization is unable to grow or broaden its fundraising efforts. However, this stereotype also applies to many men, though perhaps more often in the for-profit arena. Besides, research indicates that corporate women are generally more team-oriented than their male counterparts (Rosener, 1990).

8. *Women are interested only in special events.* We all know women who will spend hundreds of hours working on an event to raise money rather than asking for or giving the money directly. Planning and overseeing details, scheduling family members' time, and organizing meals, dinner parties, and vacations have all been an integral part of a traditional woman's résumé.

Development staff members who wish to play down the emphasis on special events must be creative to make giving and getting money just as rewarding for their female prospects and donors as planning an event.

9. *Women do not like to ask for money.* Some of the world's most successful salespeople are women, and fundraising careers are attracting more and more of them. Their success in the development field demonstrates that women can and do ask others for great amounts of money.

Volunteer fundraisers should be made aware that people *are* going to donate to charities. It is not a question of whether or not they will give but rather how much and to whom. Volunteers should also be urged not to take the job too personally.

If women do not ask for money, they will not be asked to serve on campaign committees or in other positions of influence. They should be encouraged to step up and help determine the future of the organization.

10. *Women are too self-centered to be philanthropists.* When we look around in any upscale mall and think about how much money some women spend on clothes, cosmetics, and jewelry, it can be difficult to reconcile this with the fact that women give less than men. However, more women give to charity than men (Tiehen and Andreoni, 1993), and they are deeply committed to improving society. It is up to fundraisers to convince women that philanthropy is the expression of women (and men) who feel and act as part of the community.

11. *Women try to interject their "feminist dogma" into everything.* Women who were active in the women's movement of the 1960s do sometimes find it difficult to compromise. The battle scars they received in fighting for the Equal Rights Amendment, Title IX, affirmative action, and equal pay for equal work have created a generation of women who view themselves as the smug inventors of women's issues.

Traditional organizations that wish to attract these women as donors must help them see how they can operate within the organization. One way is by establishing programs that address the issues of justice for women. Another is to draw their attention to positive role models, such as Katherine Lyall, president of the University of Wisconsin system; Donna Shalala, U.S. secretary of health and human services; Elizabeth Dole, president of the Red Cross; and Ellen Malcolm of Emily's List. In describing why she was not inter-

ested in becoming part of a political party dedicated solely to
women's issues, Malcolm said: "I want women to be powerful players in the middle, not just a fringe element" (Friedman, 1993, pp.
64–65).

Other Barriers to Women's Giving

Many women brought up in a society where men control money
not surprisingly develop some insecurity when it comes to managing their own finances and taking risks with their wealth. Development officers can help educate women about how best to invest
their money for their own future and that of society. Focus groups
and other studies have revealed certain characteristics common to
many women that present barriers to the development of their philanthropy. Let us look at seven of them.

1. *Fear of the future: the "bag lady syndrome."* When thinking
about retirement, women indicated in a recent Gallup poll that
their greatest fears had to do with financial issues, such as having
an adequate cash flow, enough money to do what they want, or simply enough to make ends meet. Women's concern for these matters
scored 22 percent higher than men's, in part no doubt because
women live an average of seven years longer than men ("Finance:
Investments . . . ," 1993, p. 4).

Older women, having lived through the Great Depression, have
a particular dread of losing everything and ending up on the street,
living out of bags, or becoming a burden to their children. According to Tracy Gary of Resourceful Women, this fear is common even
among the wealthy women she works with. It is not surprising,
therefore, that these women are reluctant to commit to a donation.

It is important to understand this fear when discussing money
with a woman, and it is helpful to have her verbalize it. Simply talking about it removes some of the worry. Bequests and trusts are ideal
for the older woman who wants to ensure her own security while at

the same time guaranteeing that the organization she cares about deeply continues to receive her support during her lifetime and after her death.

Concern about financial security may be a generational issue that will lessen as women become more comfortable with their ability to earn a living.

2. *Unfamiliarity with financial matters.* As many as 90 percent of all women will be solely responsible for their finances at some point in their lives. However, on a daily basis, most women's responsibility involves no more than balancing the checkbook and paying the bills. According to a survey on women and investment conducted by the Withlin Group for Oppenheimer Management, only about 12 percent of women actually make their own investments. Even so, Oppenheimer president Bridget A. Macaskill believes that this will change and says, "We think the survey points to an era of much broader financial involvement for women. Women have the smarts, the disposition, and the confidence to invest successfully; what they've lacked is the experience" ("Finance: Investments . . . ," 1993, p. 4).

Women's knowledge about money and investments is, by their own admission, less than that of men. Generally, women are much less secure about making financial decisions. When Susan Davis was a financial manager with Harris Bank in the early 1980s, she found that it took women ten times as long as men to make a decision concerning their finances. Yet despite the length of their deliberation, they tended to involve ten other women in the process once they made the decision. Just consider what this could mean to philanthropy! Just like women and their investments, it may take longer to cultivate a donor, but when she comes, she might well bring along a number of her friends to your organization or institution.

Women are increasingly being provided opportunities to become informed about financial matters through magazine and newspaper articles, as well as special programs offered by women's groups, banks, insurance companies, nonprofits, and other groups that share a stake in the growing potential of women as investors. By helping women become financially literate and offering projects that interest them, nonprofits can empower them to realize their full potential as investors in our institutions' success.

3. *Difficulty accepting the responsibility and power associated with money*. This may be the most complex issue of all when working with women and money. Portland philanthropist Harriet Denison suggests that many women have witnessed the power of money to destroy initiative and divide siblings in their own families and do not want anything to do with this abusive force. Atlanta philanthropist Mary Gellerstedt points out that women, who have traditionally been the peacekeepers, know that money is one item guaranteed to stir everyone up. Other women have seen how family money has been used to pollute the earth and impoverish people, and they may harbor feelings of guilt about inherited money made at the expense of others. For many women, societal pressures, religion, or a history of dependency have made them reluctant to assume responsibility for their money and the power it confers.

"By placing ourselves at a distance from the power and obligation inherent in wealth, we make its responsible use someone else's problem," says Keller Cushing Freeman. "Traditionally, we have viewed the stewardship of wealth as a masculine obligation . . . [because] for most of recorded history, women have been dealt out of the power game. We have not had access to the mechanisms by which wealth is acquired, so we have had little claim to a voice in how wealth is distributed" (Freeman, 1992, pp. 40, 41).

When women do not lay claim to the power in money, they cede the responsibility to others, along with the ability to use money to leverage action.

A redefinition of power may be in order. Instead of describing it in terms of avarice and domination, it should be interpreted by women as the energy and ability to do good things and make the world a better place. This redefinition is possible when we work directly with women to show them how their money can be used responsibly for things that are important to them. Appealing to a woman's entrepreneurial sense is another way to address the money-as-power issue. Women like to make things, and with their money they can do just that. This is an example of a responsible use of the power of money.

4. *Discouragement of female giving by "male bastions."* Women, particularly those at midlife who have made their own way in a career, frequently think twice about underwriting schools or organizations that may have discouraged or patronized them in their youth. Even if the institution abandons sexist policies and practices, many women cannot forgive and forget. One midwestern university had a male-only marching band until the mid 1960s. Although the group has admitted women for thirty years now, a female graduate was nonetheless indignant at being asked to contribute financially to a band that she had been forbidden to participate in during her years at the school.

Institutions that wish to overcome this barrier must bring to the woman's attention the gains that have been made in opportunities for women. One compelling way to do this is to have a young woman currently active in the institution meet personally with the prospect. The two could talk about how the older woman paved the way for the younger one, who is continuing to work to improve conditions for women.

A case can be made that in some instances, former male bastions are still reluctant to have women become involved, even as major donors. These organizations may be surprised someday by a "hostile takeover." When women realize their potential and work to change these groups, they *will* change them with their money and their clout.

5. *A desire for anonymity.* To be anonymous is to be a woman, according to Virginia Woolf. Many women have been taught that it is ill-mannered to call attention to themselves. Others would prefer anonymity but realize that they must serve as role models and so agree to take credit if it furthers the cause of women. As Lindsay Morganthaler, a Cleveland philanthropist, remarked, "I know I have a leadership role, which is, 'I care, so I give.' Otherwise, I would probably remain anonymous. But being visible is important when I am recruiting others."

Only by encouraging role models in our institutions and organizations will we be able to break this barrier down. Fortunately, more women are coming to understand the importance of publicizing their gifts and, when asked to do so, will allow their names to be used. This is something that we must actively ask for, however, as most women will not suggest it on their own.

6. *Spontaneous versus planned giving.* Women tend to give out of their expendable income or sit down to write a check the moment they are moved by an issue. They do little in the way of strategic giving. Women should analyze their giving from year to year, something Tracy Gary and Resourceful Women are working on, as described in Chapter Twelve. By helping women analyze where their donations went last year and their current values and interests, we can empower them to give to make a difference.

7. *Lack of image as philanthropists.* Women who do not wish to stand out generally do not discuss their giving with their peers or think of themselves as philanthropists. Though they may enjoy talking about the amount of volunteer time they give, they avoid discussing the dollar amounts they donate.

Keller Cushing Freeman says that women "have traditionally viewed the stewardship of wealth as a masculine obligation." She recounts an instance when she and her husband were asked to write separate checks to two community groups. She was shocked to learn that her husband's check was for precisely fifty times the amount of hers. She summed up the problem succinctly: "He gave out of his set of philanthropic assumptions, and I gave out of mine" (Freeman, 1992, p. 41).

Development staff and volunteer fundraisers can raise women's sights by encouraging them to discuss philanthropy. When we begin our focus groups, we usually recruit women who have never seriously considered philanthropy and do not think of themselves as philanthropists. As our discussions continue, however, the women realize that philanthropy *is* something that involves them personally. To encourage women to become involved, institutions and organizations can use focus groups, as described in Chapter Nine. After the women have considered why women give, what solicitations work best, what their values are, and how they learned about philanthropy, they can be asked to participate in more detailed discussions about planning their giving.

Freeman believes that "women themselves must claim equal philanthropic responsibility and give at the highest level of their capacity" (personal communication). One option is for wealthy families to give women equal access to family resources for the purpose of philanthropy. Once women understand what has been holding them back and how to deal with their insecurities about money, power, and themselves, they can overcome these barriers and take their rightful place in the world of philanthropy.

Chapter Six

Developing a Gender-Sensitive Fundraising Program

This chapter is designed to help you do any or all of the following things: make a major commitment to involve more women in your organization, develop female leaders and role models, increase the number of women donors and volunteer fundraisers, and take an initial few steps before trying a major program.

In the following pages we outline an eight-point program to increase your institution's appreciation of women's potential, with specific tips to help realize that potential. The use of any number of these will ensure some success in creating an awareness, not only of the present and future capacity of women's giving, but also of what women have contributed to your organization in the past. Even more important, you will be planting the seeds for a larger program by taking one step at a time—a series of steps that will educate leaders and administrators about what needs to be done.

1. *Quantify women's giving over the past five years.* Very few organizations have done this, and most are surprised to realize how much money women are already giving without any special programs or expectations from the organization. For your annual appeal or capital campaign, we suggest running the following statistics:

- Total number of students or members, male and female
- Total number of living alumni, male and female
- Total number of gifts, from men and from women

- Total gift dollars, from men and from women
- Levels of giving by women and by men, including number of gifts, dollars given, major gift club membership, and average gift size
- Percentage of female prospects on the tracking system

When we present seminars for development staff at educational institutions, we ask them to provide statistics on their women alumnae. Some typical results of this kind of analysis are exemplified by the findings of Case Western Reserve University, which revealed in 1992 that 43 percent of current gifts were from women, but only 26 percent of the prospects being tracked for the capital campaign were women.

Southwestern University, a small liberal arts college in Georgetown, Texas, in a 1992 survey determined that 54 percent of its active alumni and 34 percent of its donors were women, but only 10 percent of its volunteer leaders or prospects for the capital campaign were women.

And in 1991, donor research at the University of Wisconsin, Madison, pointed out that 50 percent of the student body and 40 percent of alumni were female and that women made up 39 percent of the total donors and 36 percent of the dollars but that women represented only 27 percent of prospect tracking in the $435 million capital campaign.

This story is repeated again and again in other institutions and organizations. We are apparently not paying attention to what women are currently giving or are capable of giving. More women are giving than are being tracked and asked, and women are not represented equitably within the organization. Just imagine the possibilities if our campaigns targeted women to the degree they already give or, even better, to the degree in which they are represented in the membership, alumni, or student body.

Because the people who give at the upper levels are generally too busy or too elderly to serve on boards, mid-level, middle-aged donors are often chosen. Unfortunately, women donors tend to be represented in the upper and lower levels but not the middle and hence are overlooked in the leadership recruitment process. As we work to cultivate more female donors, it is important to concentrate our efforts on increasing lower-level gifts and bringing them up to the mid level, where they will be noticed.

2. *Review donor acknowledgment.* Karen Stone, formerly director of special gifts at UCLA, says, "The same care and sensitivity that we bring to understanding what women are interested in giving to, and attracting their support, must also be given to the equally important acknowledgment and stewardship process as well" (personal communication).

When money comes into our organizations, we frequently assume that because both husband's and wife's names appear on the check heading, the donation is from them both or, even worse, just from the male. This often happens even when the wife is the member of the organization or graduate of the institution and sometimes when she alone has been solicited. Wrongly crediting the gift to the male not only skews the statistics but also leads to embarrassing and unfortunate mistakes. For example, when you run lists of donors to invite to cultivation or recognition events, a woman donor's name may not show up, even though she may be the family's primary philanthropic decision maker.

Fundraisers need to pay close attention to records and make sure they know which partner is the constituent, which was actually solicited, which made the donation, and how the donor wishes to be acknowledged. While many women still favor being listed by their husband's name, others prefer to use their own name. It is always better to ask the donor's preference than to guess.

When donor names are permanently etched on a building, these details are even more important. For example, a philanthropist we spoke with once gave a major university money for a building in memory of her parents. Without consulting her, the advancement office listed the donor as "Mr. and Mrs. Donor." Five years later, a divorce occurred. Mr. Donor remarried, and a new Mrs. Donor emerged, causing some confusion about which woman was the contributor. The philanthropist felt that she should have been asked about the recognition when the gift was received. The irony of this story is that when the university launched a capital campaign in the late 1980s, it returned to the woman for a seven-figure lead gift. She put up the money, and the original plaque was removed, thereby giving new meaning to the expression "leveraged gift."

3. *Examine your record-keeping methods and gift coding.* Is your computer system gender-friendly? Can you credit men and women individually as well as in couples? UCLA lets the donor determine the credit for each gift by using reply cards that ask donors to specify how they want their contributions acknowledged: "This contribution should be recorded as a gift from: Mr., Ms., or Mr. and Mrs." Other designations could be Dr., Dr. and Mrs., or Dr. and Mr. "He," "she," or "both" appears on the computer printout in the donor identification column, allowing information about men's and women's donations to be easily computed.

4. *Review your development office's standard operating procedures.* When you telephone to set up a call with a male prospect whom you know is married, do you ask if his wife will be there also? A meeting at the husband's office may prove difficult for the wife to attend if she works elsewhere or the family lives some distance away. Suggest meeting someplace in between or at their home in the evening. This works to your advantage, as well as theirs, as you are able to establish a relationship with both parties, rather than just the husband. And because women tend to outlive their spouses, establishing a relationship with the wife early on means that you can more easily continue the relationship after the husband's death.

Here is an illustration of the importance of keeping both spouses informed and involved. A farmer had long been a major gift giver to a large midwestern university. Unfortunately, he was the university's only contact in the family. When he died and left his considerable estate to his wife, no one in the development office knew the wife well enough to feel comfortable calling on her. Twelve years have passed, and now it is too late to correct the mistake. "Couple calls" earlier on would have made friends of both partners, and the relationship with the widow could have continued after the husband's death.

5. *Research and publicize several large gifts made to your organization or institution by women.* Southwestern University was surprised to discover that its largest donation ever had come from a woman. Elizabeth Wiess had actually saved the university from bankruptcy during the Great Depression, yet she remained unknown to the development staff until women's gifts were investigated for a workshop on women and philanthropy. Wiess imposed some interesting conditions on her gift, including the stipulations that no present asset of the university be used in the payment of debts, that there be no public campaign, and that an additional $40,000 be raised in less than two months. Her conditions were met.

Recognizing women's past and current contributions will not only give women a sense of pride for having made a difference in an organization but will also provide examples for today's generation of female philanthropists.

All gifts should be publicized by the institution in its materials on an ongoing basis. An annual event could also be held to recognize women's contributions and encourage other women to give. This kind of celebration is both popular and entertaining—confirming the idea that giving money can be fun.

6. *Examine your boards and campaign leadership and the ways in which members are recruited.* Female prospects look carefully at board composition as an indication of an institution's commitment to gender equity. If they find that the numbers are not proportionate, they

may decide against a major gift. So it is worth your time to look at the composition of your boards and committees. What percentage of the members is women? Do the numbers reflect the proportion of women involved with your organization or institution as members, students, alumni, and donors?

If a board is male-dominated, it might be worthwhile to look at how the members are recruited. Do they generally come from a few organizations, such as downtown or professional clubs, which themselves may tend to have few female members? It would be wise to recruit from other groups, such as women's organizations, as well.

Are you recruiting your boards from top executive positions in corporations? With only 19 women directors and executives and 3,993 men at 799 major companies, it will be very difficult to find female candidates in these ranks (Schmittroth, 1991, p. 27).

Do you look for gift-giving performance or potential when seeking board members? As we have noted, you will probably be excluding women if you use this criterion because women tend not to give in the middle levels. It may be necessary for you to look at a woman's potential and what she is capable of giving rather than what she has given.

Do you have only one or two women involved at the top levels and consider that adequate? Women regard this as tokenism, almost as insulting as not having any women at all. Scanty representation makes it appear that few competent female candidates are available.

Often there is no intentional bias in choosing board members. It may simply be that the predominantly male leaders tend to choose people they are most comfortable working with—people like themselves. It may just take reminders on the part of both genders in leadership positions to ensure that women are included to the same extent as they are represented in the general population.

Women should also be included in campaign leadership. More female prospects would surely be identified and asked to give if there were more women on campaign committees suggesting the names of likely candidates.

7. *Call on women and ask them to give.* One of our colleagues at a Big Ten university questions whether men and women should be approached for gifts differently. Even so, she has targeted women for 50 percent of her calls. If we all did that, it would make an incredible difference in the sums raised from women. Time and again we hear women saying that they are simply not asked to give. We must help women take their place in philanthropy by offering them the opportunity.

Given women's special values and interests, think of how very different our institutions and organizations might be if more women contributed major gifts to the programs they care about. Children, day care, the environment, education—these causes would move ahead with the traditional male-supported projects, such as the technology, business, and athletic programs that are more generously supported today.

8. *Apply female communication methods when making major gift calls on women.* Considering that the standard fundraising call was designed by men to be used with other men, it is important to learn women's styles of communication and apply them when calling on women. New techniques will help put women at ease during a call and will also increase your likelihood of success.

A colleague from the University of Minnesota attended a session called "Women and Philanthropy: Changing the Paradigm" that we presented with Joan Fisher, director of development of B'nai B'rith Women, at the National Society of Fundraising Executives' 1992 international conference in San Francisco. The session included training in gender differences in communications. During the next year, the Minnesota colleague applied some of our methods with female donors and elicited a million-dollar gift from a woman for an endowed research chair in women's athletics. Another colleague, a man who raises money for the Girl Scouts, said at the San Francisco conference that he has to consciously avoid using male communication methods when dealing with women.

Certain skills are important in communicating with women prospects and donors:

- Build rapport and establish a connection by personalizing the call. Find out about the potential donor, and tell her a little about yourself. Find out what her interests are, and talk about her connection to your organization. Then discuss the cause.

- Be a good listener, and maintain eye contact. Listening is the most important communication skill, and all skillful fundraisers listen far more than they talk.

- Do not use peer pressure to get her to commit to a gift. Telling one prospect that another has given a certain amount and asking for a matching gift or greater may work well with men, but it is usually ineffective—and may even be detrimental—with women. A far better way is to ask her to join with others to help make a difference in the organization.

- Continue the connection and provide accountability, even after the close. Time and again we heard from women donors that they were not thanked or recognized often enough after making gifts, were not kept informed about their gift's use, and were not provided with accountability details. Thank-you notes and updates are important to everyone, but especially to women who take good manners seriously.

By examining how your development office operates and how women have responded philanthropically, you can get a good idea of how your female donors and prospects view your organization. With all the competing forces out there for the philanthropic dollar, no organization can afford to overlook women donors or, worse, drive them away. All development staff should be trained in how to communicate with both men and women effectively. Raising the gender sensitivity of the department will attract more women donors, who will be delighted by the fact that you value their opinions and their participation. In a world of male-dominated institutions, yours will stand out for its enlightened views and will draw loyal women supporters.

Chapter Seven

Communicating with Women

Development work revolves around communication. Whether with images, words, or actions, we communicate a message to our donors and prospects. That message has traditionally been created by men for men. However, the new market of the female donor brings with it fresh and innovative styles of communication. As we suggested in Chapter Six, development officers would be wise to adjust their standard approach to meet these new prospects on their own terms.

This chapter highlights the unique ways in which women communicate and the kinds of communication they respond to. It draws on the well-researched strategies that corporations and their advertisers have developed to appeal to female consumers. Development professionals have much to learn from these companies, which have spent millions of dollars to find out how to tap this lucrative new market.

Knowing the Market

Advertisers are finding that today's woman does not easily fit into a single category. "There is no way of saying to women today, 'This is you,'" explains Helayne Spivak, executive vice president and executive creative director of the Young and Rubicam advertising agency (Pomice, 1993, p. 104). As a result, advertisers are scrambling to keep up with women, to capture and reflect the changes that they are undergoing. Advertising strategies of past decades that attempted to provoke or tease women into buying products are being replaced by images that appeal to a more complicated consumer.

For example, women's magazines are using images based on demographic and psychological profiles of their readers. Some see their readers as educated, intelligent, and affluent. Frances Lear, editor in chief of *Lear's*, said, "We have great hopes for what [the reader] can do for herself and for her community" (Krafft, 1991, p. 50). Publishers know that during the next decade, there will be a huge increase of aging baby boomer women, and some magazines are preparing to meet the challenge (Krafft, 1991, p. 50).

Newspapers, too, have discovered in their efforts to win back women readers that it is difficult to target as a single entity a group as diverse as women (Pearl, 1992, p. B1). Nonprofits can resolve the problems inherent in addressing such a diverse group by singling out subgroups by age and developing programs for each subgroup. Young career women and homemakers might wish to have a lunch group whose purposes range from mentoring girls and financial education to fundraising. A slightly older group might want to take fundraising more seriously, provide leadership training for other women, and become sophisticated about the financial advantages of philanthropy. An older women's group might raise funds and discover the thrill and advantages of giving gifts themselves.

Like corporate marketers, nonprofits can collect demographic data about their women donors, categorizing donors by age and viewpoint. Development officers can then use this profile information when communicating with female prospects in person and in writing.

Many of today's older women donors lead very active lives that are vastly different from those of their mothers a generation ago. They are busier, healthier, and more tolerant of change as they observe their children, who are themselves breaking new ground in lifestyles, relationships, and family structures. This may influence their decisions about giving, and as we communicate with these new older women, who represent the majority of our major female donors, we might be surprised by what they will support. Although they may have supported traditional projects in the past, many of these women now have other areas of greater concern based on the experiences of their own children and grandchildren. For example, they may be receptive to programs advancing women in nontraditional careers, as well as projects supporting day care and early childhood education.

Other development opportunities exist for younger female prospects, provided that we understand what their interests are and where they stand in their life process. Rena Bartos, of the J. Walter Thompson advertising agency, suggests that we constantly reexamine the target group, noting that attitudes, values, and lifestyles are in flux for many women. The late thirties through mid forties are for many women a time of reevaluation, which can signal changes in priorities (Nichols, 1990a, p. 94). For example, many women in their forties are beginning to recognize the need for financial planning for retirement and are receptive to looking at planned-giving vehicles.

Designated funds are an option for women who are in the midst of educating their children and do not have a great deal of expendable income. This fund could represent a pledge over a certain period of time with the principle growing for twenty years, after which the fund would begin to generate income for grants to programs of the donor's choice. The Milwaukee Foundation has found this to be a successful tool for its younger career women donors.

What Is the Best Approach?

Again, we can take our lead from what magazines are doing to approach their female readers. Susan Krafft, associate editor of *American Demographics*, lists some ways in which magazines are communicating with women, including speaking in a thoughtful and sensible manner, having a caring nature, and looking for solutions and strategies for living (Krafft, 1991, pp. 47, 50). As we discuss our programs and strategies with donors and prospects, it is important to keep these factors in mind and be prepared to elaborate the reasons why our program is crucial. Further questions may arise and should be considered beforehand: why the program is or is not a collaborative effort, whom it can help, and how it might make the world a better place.

According to Judith Nichols, a marketing specialist and fundraising consultant, the approach used to target women in institutional publications should also take into account the colors and kinds of graphics women prefer. She advises using crisper copy and bolder graphics when writing for younger, career-oriented women. By contrast, subdued colors, graphics, and copy appeal more to the traditional older woman (Nichols, 1990a, p. 96).

As we approach our older women donors in particular, it may appear easier to employ charm in place of a respectful appeal and a realistic message that can help empower them as philanthropists. Indeed, pleasantries are important, but nonprofits need donors and prospects who are capable of making their own well-thought-out decisions about our programs. Just as advertisers are keeping in mind the term *respect* when directing their message to women, development officers should also communicate respect and honesty when approaching donors.

We can also learn from the marketers of women's clothing. For example, in 1989, Nike used superstar female athletes to attract more women's business—an approach that had previously proved successful with male consumers, who had rushed to buy shoes endorsed by superstar male basketball players. Kate Bednarski, manager for Nike's women's division, admits, however, that the campaign that attempted to make a hero out of triathlete Joanne Ernst "was a flop. Customers said: 'You make great men's stuff, but I don't feel you understand me'" (Zinn, 1991, p. 90).

This initial failure led to the now famous $12 million campaign created to show that Nike *did* understand women, including their fears and aggravations. The winning campaign stresses building self-esteem through exercise and urges women to accept themselves as they are rather than try to achieve superhuman physical perfection (Pomice, 1993, p. 105). The Nike campaign focuses on building a relationship with women through honest and straightforward talk, the kind you would have with your best friend.

This female-oriented approach has been a major success for Nike. The company's sales to women jumped 25 percent in 1990, the first full year of the campaign. They grew by another 25 percent in 1991 and by 28 percent in 1992, making sales to women one of the company's fastest-growing segments (Pomice, 1993, p. 130).

The incredible success of this campaign came from a radically different advertising approach, as well as the increased production of clothes and shoes. Translating that to development is easy. If we target more women respectfully and realistically through our media efforts and then follow up with calls, the results we see in gifts from female donors could double in five years, as Nike's sales did.

Incorporating Women's Values in Our Programs

Our research into women's values and how they relate to philanthropy has been corroborated in a report by Dyan Sublett and Karen Stone of UCLA on focus groups held in 1992. Some of the most important conclusions are that women give from the heart, that they give to make a difference, and that they want the world to be a better place in which to bring up children (Sublett and Stone, 1993, pp. 4–6).

When we look at advertisers' interpretations of women's values, we see many of these same themes represented in the photos and copy emphasizing children, women and girls, diversity, and the environment. For example, the upscale designer Donna Karan crafted a campaign in 1992 that portrayed a young woman running for and winning the U.S. presidency. Karan told *Working Woman* that the next segment of the ad campaign would show the woman doing her job as president. "Maybe she'll be working with children," says Karan. "Maybe with the homeless. Maybe she'll be dealing with the environment. Whatever it is, she's got to be actually doing something, making a real difference" (Clarke, 1992, p. 15).

Toyota has been effectively reaching out to women through its ads, which present themes of nurturing and diversity, helping women and girls, and developing relationships. One ad for the "I love what you do for me" campaign focuses on relationships by showing a woman standing with other women beside a Toyota. The headline reads "This Could Be the Start of a Beautiful Relationship." Another ad for the campaign, "Investing in the Individual," appeared in the *Wall Street Journal*. It features a young woman of color who had received a scholarship from the company through the United Negro College Fund. Thanks in part to these campaigns, more than 60 percent of Toyotas are purchased by women.

Fundraisers, too, must frequently reassess programs and messages to continue to address issues that women consider important. Do our programs offer women choices and positions of influence in areas that will interest them and make a difference? If so, are we adequately conveying the message about these values in our publications and our calls?

As professionals, we should also be aware of the programs within our organizations and institutions that promote multiculturalism and help address social problems. By publicizing these programs, we give women an opportunity to participate and support efforts for change. In some cases, this may mean setting up new projects so that women can be involved from the beginning. Such an opportunity to share in the creation of something has enormous appeal to many women.

Perhaps the issues and values that women feel most strongly about—safety features in automobiles, for example—will become mainstream within our organizations in the same way they have the auto industry. Perhaps, through our collective voice and our philanthropy, we will focus our institutions on those things that women care about: children, the elderly, health care, and education.

Addressing and Correcting Past Mistakes

Companies facing the biggest challenge in marketing to women are those that spent years alienating them. *Business Week* reporter Laura Zinn says, "Many traditional beer ads have offended women with scenes of beer-guzzling men ogling bikini-clad beach bunnies." She relates how Anheuser-Busch has begun to correct this kind of advertising, which confuses sensuality with sexual exploitation. Steve Burrows, the company's vice president of beer brand management, says, "We certainly haven't offended women intentionally; we have listened, and where change was appropriate, we were willing to change" (Zinn, 1991, p. 86).

It is often easy to believe that coeducational campuses have always been fully integrated in terms of gender. But in truth, not many years have passed since women have been permitted to participate fully on most campuses. Many activities have only recently been opened, including university bands and athletic teams. Complex and challenging problems exist for institutions that once excluded women from their boards or made female student life trying. As development officers, we need to be aware of our institutions' past practices when communicating with women. Programs, committees, boards, and other groups that exclude women should be opened up, and the progress that women have made in the institution should be communicated to all female prospects.

Communicating an Institution's Image

Sprint/United Telecom publicizes its outstanding record as an equal opportunity employer through a campaign titled "It's a New World." An ad for this campaign in an executive women's magazine says, "After looking into our hiring practices, leading civil rights groups decided to make an example of us."

The first step in evaluating the image that an institution communicates in its publications is uncomplicated. The editors of the

Chicago Tribune employed it a couple of years ago in assessing that paper's appeal to women. They simply counted the number of photos and articles that included women in the daily paper (Pearl, 1992, p. B1). This is something that nonprofits can do just as effortlessly. A periodic review of photos and features in our publications to ensure that they include a good representation of women will help create an image of an institution committed to women's values and interests.

A more complex but also more substantive approach is an examination of the numbers of women on our boards and in administration. This reveals how women fit into the institution's long-range plans, programs, and fundraising efforts, as well as its commitment to engaging and involving women. A transformation in this arena will likely require many hours and much effort, but in addition to tapping the talents and expertise of both halves of the population, it has the added benefit of generating positive material for press releases and publications reporting the progress of the restructuring. In addition, there is no better way of presenting an institution's concern for women than by featuring female donors in regular publications.

Finally, individually, as development officers, we need to be aware of how we present ourselves when speaking for the institution. We should consider how we engage our donors; how we cultivate our prospects and ask for gifts; what we ask for; how we thank and acknowledge donors; how we identify, recruit, and recognize volunteers; and how we "add value" to those agreeing to be involved. Are we limiting ourselves to suggesting tickets to a football game or an afternoon of golf? Or have we looked into what our women donors might be interested in and made those perks available too?

Communicating the Image of Women

The challenge today is to represent women in publications who look like real people, people to whom our donors can relate.

The Toyota campaign depicts women's diversity by showing

women of color, women playing team sports, and working women with families. CIBA-Geigy's Estraderm campaign highlights older women who are still active and attractive. Even some swimwear fashions are now being modeled by mature women.

One direct-mail production company specializing in planned giving usually does a good job of preparing materials aimed at women but made the mistake of using photos of national media personalities in its four-color brochures. It is difficult for the average person to believe that what Connie Chung or Katherine Graham does has much relevance to her own life. The production company might better have suggested that institutions and organizations use photos of their own female donors.

Images go beyond photos and drawings. The images of women we present in our promotional materials must also be realistic and depict the complexities of women's lives and the balance that they try to achieve—a balance that may involve home, children, parents, career, friends, partner, and recreation. Just as advertisers are seeing the necessity of presenting multifaceted images of American women that accurately portray their many roles and responsibilities, our organizations must also be sure to reflect women's diversity realistically in all publications.

Communicating Appreciation for Women's Special Values

Corporations like Dean Witter are using advertising in women's magazines to acknowledge the contribution of women to their professions and communities. They credit women's long-standing role as volunteers and professionals through ads like the one headed "We're Looking for Dedicated People like Renee Nourse." The ad goes on to explain that Nourse has a tremendous sense of community responsibility, demonstrated through her dedication to a local social service organization for which she works as a board member and financial officer.

Sara Lee Corporation annually takes out a full page ad in the

New York Times and other major publications to showcase its Front Runner Awards, given to women who best embody the "qualities of strength, balance, and integrity." The ad proclaims, "We admire their accomplishments. We share their spirit. We celebrate their lives." Through these awards, Sara Lee recognizes the value of women's emotional strength and integrity and their capacity to balance work and family.

In the nonprofit world, women tend to volunteer before they give, and our institutions should recognize this important commitment. Acknowledging women's voluntary contributions, as well as their financial ones, tells them that their efforts are important and that we value them.

We, too, might give awards to women who volunteer, recognizing not only the woman's contribution to the organization but also other work she does at home and in the community. What better way to show that we understand a woman's various and dynamic roles in today's society and are grateful that she has chosen to volunteer for our organization?

Advantages of Women Communicating with Women

Do women communicate better with other women than with men? Mazda Motor of America, Inc., thinks so. A woman serves as marketing vice president for the company's Mazda division. Jan Thompson, the highest-ranking woman in auto sales, is focusing her efforts on women. Besides marketing to women through ads, Thompson has also expanded the company's sponsorship of women's golf and tennis and has set up golf clinics that raise money for the Susan G. Komen Breast Cancer Foundation (Armstrong, 1992).

Women are flocking to development careers today, just as they are to marketing and advertising jobs. At the Wharton School, 24 percent of all 1992 female graduates went into marketing, versus 13 percent of men. The numbers of women choosing careers in advancement continue to rise, and women now represent 58 percent of the total profession. As in corporate advertising, women in development are clustered in middle management, but as their numbers increase, this is likely to change for both professions (Pomice, 1993, p. 106; Tifft, 1992, pp. 66, 68).

Maidenform's Marilyn Bane believes that women bring something special to advertising: "The nerve endings are out there just a little bit further. It's an empathy you can't expect someone to have who hasn't gone through what you have" (personal communication). As more women enter positions in which they help plan and implement fundraising messages, they can use their female communication skills to make a difference on solicitations and publications.

One of the most important factors of communication is the ability to ask questions, and according to Marjorie David, founding editor of the Sunday *Chicago Tribune*'s "Womanews" section, women do this better than men. "There is a difference in the kinds of questions men and women ask in covering stories," she says. "A man doesn't think of asking women what they think. Women touch on relationships. They want the facts too, but they also want to know how people feel about what is happening" (personal communication).

Women represent a whole new prospect market, one that female development officers are particularly well equipped to target because of their shared gender. This unique position gives women an advantage and a responsibility. It is up to us to target female prospects with an appeal that will interest them, as well as to portray them accurately in our publications.

Effective Communication Techniques

A giant in clothing manufacturing, Liz Claiborne says that the company seldom makes a move without first listening to its customers. She employs about 150 specialists at stores around the country to solicit feedback from customers, and she is willing to make changes based on the customers' responses. "This is a painfully honest company," says Wendy Banks, the company's senior vice president of marketing. "We take responsibility for our mistakes, and then we learn and go forward" (Better, 1992).

It is important that development officers, too, study the ways in which other sectors of the business community are accommodating, and sometimes promoting, the changes in society. We must ask questions of our women donors and be willing to change things that are not working.

To demonstrate interest in our female prospects and gain valuable information about our organizations, we should watch for opportunities to ask open-ended questions: May I ask you a few questions about how you see this organization? How do you see yourself relating to this project? Do you have any questions you would like to ask of me? Is there anything further I can provide for you? Focus groups are particularly engaging to women and are being used extensively by advertising agencies to determine attributes women look for in their products.

Focus groups are also being employed in the "new capital campaign," as outlined in Chapter Ten. Up to this point, women have generally been ignored in capital campaigns, either due to old stereotypes about women's giving or simply because men were making the leadership selections. This is a new era, however, and the influence of women will change the structure of campaigns.

New Ways of Communicating

There are many points of similarity between the nonprofit world and the advertising industry. Both endeavors are always in need of more clients, prospects, customers, or donors. Both are always searching out new ways to tell a story. Both rely heavily on image when developing an approach, and changes in lifestyle and people's values affect both industries strongly. Finally, advertisers and fundraisers alike are always striving to "catch up" with what is going on in the world so as to define and communicate our message more effectively. By watching and learning from new communication methods that have been developed in the advertising industry, non-profit development officers can take the best of the strategies and deploy them in the fundraising arena.

Part Three

Women and Major Gifts

Chapter Eight

Developing a Comprehensive Plan for Involving Women as Leaders and Donors

All or any of the suggestions in Chapter Six will help attract more women to an organization as participants, leaders, and donors. But a longer-lasting commitment would be to establish a program that includes all eight of the items described within the context of a structured and organized process. This will take a great deal more time and effort, but it is an effort well worth the while. Not only will women become more involved with your organization and contribute more dollars, but they will also bring to the table new ideas and visions that help revitalize and renew your programs and your institution as a whole.

A Complete Plan

In this chapter we lay out a complete plan for involving more women in your organization or institution. We have used parts of programs that have already proved successful. In particular, we would like to thank Mallory M. Simpson of the University of Michigan for sharing that institution's plan with us. It is one of the most completely developed programs we have seen, and in the following pages we have adapted it to fit other organizations.

1. *Establish a task force.* A task force representing top administrative and board leadership as well as development staff and women philanthropists should be recruited to develop the mission and goals of the program. It is helpful to hold a staff workshop on

women and philanthropy as a first step to inform the task force about the potential for such a program. The individuals on the task force, including some men, will assist in raising the organization's understanding and awareness of the issues, including the problems and challenges. They will propose a program and monitor its progress.

2. *Hold prospect gatherings to inform women about philanthropy.* Women generally enjoy getting together with one another and may be particularly responsive to an invitation to hear someone talk about the importance of their involvement. Speakers could discuss issues that women generally feel need addressing, including problems such as the status of children in today's society, the education of girls, and the environment. Each session will help women begin to explore their own attitudes about philanthropy by asking them to think about these important social issues and how they can play a part in addressing them. Speakers should discuss the positive and negative perceptions of women as donors. Finally, depending on the group, the speakers may want to ask the women how they would give away, say, $100,000 or $1 million. What type of program would they support? How would they earmark the gift? Would it be an outright donation, a deferred gift, or a challenge? Would they stipulate that certain conditions be met by the organization? These questions are very useful for stimulating people to think about philanthropy and to imagine themselves as philanthropists. This kind of discussion works nicely during a meal, with each table reporting its results before hearing the speaker's comments about women and philanthropy.

3. *Be aware of your institution's public image.* People want to see their values reflected in their institutions. Through your publications, news releases, programs, and fundraising efforts, your organization delivers a message about what it considers vital. It will be necessary to review everything that influences your public image

and continually monitor it to ensure that prospects view the organization as one that values women's participation. Here are some ways to do this:

- Review your campaign materials and other publications for references to women and women's interests.
- Count the number of women in leadership positions.
- Evaluate your programs and how they serve women.

4. *Involve staff in the program.* Male and female staff members need to understand the relevance and potential of a program designed to increase women's involvement in development. But as with most programs involving the potential for change, not everyone will be convinced. Only when the senior administrators are solidly behind the program will the staff in its entirety feel an urgency to become informed. Staff training sessions (with senior development administrators present) will sensitize staff about women's potential for advancing the organization, their interests, and the changes in operating procedures that should take place.

In the workshops we have given around the country, the topic of women's philanthropy has been received enthusiastically by development professionals and volunteers alike. They enjoy the opportunity to consider a topic that explores their own personal values and attitudes, and both women and men have been very open to discussion and learning.

We begin by asking questions to sensitize people and help them connect with the program. If they become involved at the onset, they will be more able to understand the message. Here are some samples for stimulating discussion at a staff meeting:

- What is the perception of women as major donors in your development office?
- Describe a positive experience you have had with a woman donor, and explain why it was positive.

- Describe a negative experience you have had with a woman donor, and explain why it was negative.

Assignments like these will start people thinking and wanting to know more. The important thing is to keep asking questions: What works? What does not? And why?

5. *Conduct focus groups with women.* Winning politicians used focus groups successfully in the 1992 political races. President Bill Clinton's media guru, Mandy Grunwald, helped set up what she called the Manhattan Project to test new message tracks and find out what people, mostly women, really thought about candidate Clinton. Groups of ten to twenty-six women in Pennsylvania, New Jersey, and Ohio were instrumental in the final selection of the winning campaign themes, which stressed people first and opportunity with responsibility (Goldman & Mathews, 1992).

Focus groups are very popular with women, who have too seldom been asked for their opinions. In fact, women regard focus groups as entertainment and a way to get together with other women not only to express their views but also to hear what the others have to say. Focus groups nowadays seem to be taking the place of coffees, luncheons, and receptions because they recognize the importance of women's values, help raise consciousness, and build self-confidence.

The sessions can be formal and structured, led by professional moderators, or conducted informally by staff. The most important point is that the person conducting the dialogues be a good listener and a conversation facilitator. If you are trying to determine women's opinions of your institution, an outside facilitator might be more likely than a staff person to elicit honest and objective comments. However, our experience indicates that women are generally not afraid to speak up when invited, no matter who is doing the asking.

In either case, it is important to ask the same set of questions of each focus group if you wish to make valid comparisons. The following lists include some basic ideas to get women thinking about philanthropy and help establish their values and motivations for giving. Also included are questions about the organization itself. Indeed, women will expect to be asked about the organization and will definitely have some opinions.

The second set of questions can be used as much as six months to a year after women have become comfortable with the notion of themselves as philanthropists. At this time, they are beginning to think about larger and more complex issues of women's giving, including how to get personal assistance in planning their giving. These focus groups will help define the kinds of women's programs that might be useful within the larger organization and what the women want to get from their involvement. In general, as women delve into the subject of philanthropy, they become interested in learning more. A women's program usually needs to be a combination of continuing education about the subject and a vehicle to accomplish something for the larger organization. Just setting up an organization, however, without an evaluation of the women involved and their views on philanthropy, will make them less likely to want to include fundraising among their activities, along with networking and advising the organization's leadership. Focus groups are a powerful tool for helping women find their voice and discover their potential as philanthropists.

The process that works best for focus groups is to have no more than ten to twelve in a group, and meet for one and a half to two hours, allowing fifteen to twenty minutes for the women to mingle and get acquainted before the structured session begins. The focus groups can be held around a meal or coffee in a quiet place at a restaurant or in someone's office or home. Seating around a single table is best. Twelve questions, discussed for approximately five minutes each, allow for open discourse by everyone.

The participants can be grouped by age, interests, or any other category that makes sense to your organization. However, we can guarantee that if they know that there are other groups gathering to consider the same topics, they will be very curious about the results and will want to get together later to share information. This, of course, provides another opportunity for the staff to connect with the women and conduct a dialogue. In any case, it is imperative that the participants be informed of the results of the focus groups.

A note of caution, though: It may be easier to ask established donors, rather than prospects, to participate. Often prospects are suspicious or simply not interested. At any rate, the information that is truly useful concerns what motivates the people who already give to your organization, and that can come only from donors. Focus groups centered around issues concerning the institution itself, rather than women and philanthropy, may be a better way to involve prospects. The participants can let you know how they feel about what is going on presently within the organization and perhaps express criticisms that will help the leadership in its efforts to transform the structure of the organization to one that is more sensitive to women's values.

The facilitator should ask the questions and be prepared to give some examples or analogies. Each person at the table should have an opportunity to respond to at least the first question. This helps make people comfortable, and the dialogue can begin. Watch out for people who try to dominate the conversation. The facilitator must remain aware of how long each person is speaking and move the discussion along. Someone other than the facilitator should be designated to take extensive notes and tape-record the meetings for later transcription. Notes are extremely useful but by themselves are always incomplete.

Finally, an analysis must be prepared and presented. A twist might be to invite two people with an interest in women's issues to react to the presentation at a later session with development staff and volunteer leadership.

Questions Defining Women's Giving

What are the major issues facing our nation today?

What are the negative perceptions about women's giving?

What are the positive perceptions about women's giving?

How did you learn your philanthropy? (This gets at the importance of learning philanthropy from families.)

How do you prefer to be approached for a contribution, and why? What kind of solicitation do you like the least?

What characteristics of an organization are important to you as you make your decisions about giving?

Once you have given to an organization, how likely are you to continue giving to that same organization, and why?

What kind of recognition is important to you?

How do you make decisions about giving in your family?

How would you give away $1 million (or $100,000)?

What do you like about (your organization)? What adjectives come to mind when you think about (your institution)?

What do we need to do to improve the organization?

What information do you get about the institution, and does it match your areas of interest?

Questions Examining Whether a Separate Women's Group
Would Be of Interest

What does being a philanthropist mean to you? (Try to determine what key values and rewards women get from philanthropy.)

How do you plan your philanthropic giving? (Most women do not plan; they write checks as they are moved to give. Discuss giving to a few causes versus many and the leadership potential available with the first option that is not present with the second.)

What are your philanthropic goals this year? (Again, most women do not have clear goals in mind. Elicit responses covering broad topics like the environment, dance, children, and women.)

Will your giving this year be different from last year? (Find out to whom they gave last year.)

What do you hope to accomplish with your money during your lifetime?

At what age do women begin to think of themselves as benefactors?

What are some ways we can teach and encourage philanthropy among young women? (This issue turns out to be particularly important.)

What do you think are the major differences in the ways women of different age groups approach their giving?

Do you think that there are differences in the giving patterns between women who have inherited or married money and those who have earned it? If so, what are the differences?

Women control 60 percent of the money in the United States, yet children and women make up 75 percent of the nation's poor. How do you account for this vast difference between the haves and the have-nots?

Statistics show that women give 1.8 percent of their income to nonprofits, while men give 3.1 percent. How can we raise women's sights about giving so that they will contribute more? (This will lead into the definition of a major gift and how it may differ for women and men.)

How could you structure a gift to have an impact on an institution and to make a change? (Try to get them talking about leveraging their gift.)

Would you like a special program or council within the organization that deals with women and philanthropy? If so, what would you like it to do, and how would you want to be involved?

6. *Interview your women philanthropists.* Focus groups are important, but personal interviews are especially valuable. Administrators who may be doubting the need for a women's program will more likely be persuaded by the results of both focus groups and personal interviews. Moreover, the information gathered will be useful for your publications featuring women donors.

The same questionnaire can be used for focus groups and interviews alike, although there is more opportunity for the conversation to wander in a personal interview.

This is the interview process we suggest:

- Begin by asking a little about the woman's early life: where she grew up, where she went to school, and so on.

- Ask about her major funding interest: how she became involved, what she does for the organization in terms of time commitment (is she a volunteer fundraiser?), and what was so special about this group that led her to support it. This exploration will probably move into a discussion of her values and of what led her to become financially involved (for example, her upbringing, a divorce, illness, death of a loved one).

- Find out what she looks for in an organization or what factors are important and might motivate her to give.

- Ask about her parents: Was philanthropy important to them? What did they support? This will help get at her views regarding the importance of learning and encouraging philanthropy at an early age.

- Ask what other things she supports and why. Are there things she will not contribute to? If so, why?

- Initiate a discussion about women, power, and money to

reveal her thoughts on these subjects and the relationships among them. This is a particularly provocative area, and she will certainly have an opinion. One way to get into the subject is by talking about female political candidates in the 1992 elections and what women have accomplished by supporting women's funds over the past decade.

- Find out who else is involved in her philanthropic decision making—family members or financial advisers, for example—and the extent of their influence.

- If she is a volunteer fundraiser, find out what approaches she feels work best with female prospects and why. Ask if she applies different approaches when working with women and men and to explain them.

- Find out what approaches she personally does not care for and why.

- Ask her to cite reasons why women choose not to give or not to give more and to suggest ways in which these can be addressed.

- Find out how she feels about being an anonymous donor versus announcing her gift openly and becoming a role model.

- Ask what kind of recognition she prefers and why.

- Ask what she is planning to do for the future of her major funding interest. This will get at her planned giving and how she feels about her future in terms of her finances.

- Ask what staff can do to be more helpful to her.

7. *Develop a plan that takes women's ages and life stages into account.* There are several general categories of women prospects: the young professional or homemaker, who is not likely to be able to commit to a major gift; the new older woman, who may be able to give a major gift over ten years; and the woman who is already capable of giving a large gift. It is helpful in this area to begin by

developing profiles of your women donors using these designations or others that might be more appropriate. How women view giving and how much they give can be very much a generational issue. Establishing a plan that recognizes each of these life stages will help your organization address women's various and changing priorities.

These priorities can range from establishing a career or a home; raising children and providing for their education; retirement; old age; and widowhood. Although it would be a mistake to keep the groups entirely apart—depriving participants of the interchange of ideas and interests—there are ways to arrange interaction and still make the issues pertinent and meaningful to all. For example, seminars on planning for retirement would hardly be worthwhile for women in their seventies, but a guest speaker brought in to talk about the plight of children in America or women in the arts would be of interest to all three groups at the same time.

Some organizations would benefit from having different groups, depending on life stage and interests, or one large group with separate subgroups. The organization can be purely social or serve other functions such as fundraising, mentoring, or advising the administration. Some groups, particularly those with younger women, may get together primarily for networking, as is done at Case Western Reserve University in Cleveland. It is a shame to miss the opportunity to educate women and get them in the habit of giving while they are young. The President's Council of Cornell Women does just that by setting up subgroups, one of which raises funds.

For women who are able to give or are already major donors, particular opportunities should be arranged to keep them active in the system. Just as in any group of top donors, special measures must be taken to provide experiences with peers, whether it be in social or leadership roles.

Showing women that your organization cares about them as individuals—and will make plans that focus on their interests— communicates that they are valued and needed. This is always a prerequisite to asking for money.

8. *Educate your staff about investments.* To establish credibility with your female prospects, you have to know about finances yourself. You and your staff must be able to discuss bonds and stock market investments with confidence, as well as trusts and other deferred gifts. Although development officers and donors are not peers, fundraisers must at least be able to talk with their women donors and prospects as equals in investment knowledge. In many cases, the major gift solicitor will even have to be able to help educate a prospective donor. All of this requires financial and investment experience. For many women fundraisers, as for women donors, this will require a boost in self-confidence and some training in financial management. A 1992 nationwide survey from Oppenheimer Funds showed that 53 percent of the women surveyed said that men are more knowledgeable about investment issues than women ("Finance: Investments . . . ," 1993, p. 5). The best way to overcome this attitude and build self-confidence is to get training and practice.

9. *Conduct financial seminars for women.* Many groups have been doing this for years, but not always with good attendance. Only recently have more women begun to recognize the value of financial training. In many cases, their reluctance is tied up with negative or fearful feelings about money and power. We need to present the sessions with less focus on making money and more on opportunities to use money to help others while retaining sufficient funds to live comfortably and securely. Seminars on ways to develop planned gifts have worked well for Spelman College, according to Billie Sue Schulze, its vice president for institutional advancement.

10. *Develop a program to enhance leadership skills in women.* Serving on a board or committee generally makes people more aware of the needs of the organization and, consequently, better donors. Female board candidates should be informed, though, that board membership implies a certain level of financial commitment. Unfortunately, women have not had the opportunities for developing the essential leadership skills that men have had. This is par-

ticularly true of women who are of an age to be asked to assume leadership positions. It is best to plan a two-level program to reach older women who are ready for these positions while preparing younger women through other kinds of service.

11. *Develop special projects for which women can raise money.* This is one good way to help develop leadership and fundraising skills in women. It can be either a project where all of the money is raised by women from women or one where women do the fundraising from men as well. In either case, the project should be one that the women have chosen themselves and in which they have a particular interest. Do not make the mistake of selecting a project that you think they might like without asking them—and take nothing for granted, as they may surprise you. It is entirely possible that they will not be interested in raising money for the ballet or women's athletics or the children's ward of a hospital. It must be their call, depending on what projects are available. But remember, women like to support their friends. Once you get a few women interested, they will probably enlist the rest themselves.

12. *Train women to ask for money.* Many women say that they cannot or will not raise money. Both statements probably contain a lot of truth. But by getting women together and making the process fun, as described in Chapter Nine, you are showing them that you believe in their abilities, and you are helping them gain self-confidence and assume leadership roles. While you are educating them, you are also providing an important and continuing connection to the organization. This kind of connection is in itself very important. At the same time, training women to ask for money, particularly from women they know, will increase both the prospect pool and the total amount of dollars raised.

13. *Assign resources to the program, and recognize the time and effort involved.* It is inconsistent to say that you support a program encouraging women and philanthropy and then not assign suffi-

cient resources to bring the program to life. Both staff and money are needed to ensure that sufficient attention is devoted to the effort and that it does not end up as yet another assignment tacked onto one person's busy schedule. Also, donors and prospects will not perceive the program as important if they do not see money and staff involved. Attention and resources will ensure that it is not referred to as "that little women's project."

As with planned gifts, this kind of program requires education and takes time, facts that people must be made aware of from the beginning. There may be some surprises, but women generally need to think of themselves as philanthropists before they can be expected to become major gift givers. Although rewarding, the process of raising women's sights as philanthropists can be lengthy.

14. *Publicize your efforts.* To demonstrate your dedication to setting up a program, publicize what you are doing. This will show that you are serious and will motivate female prospects and donors to become involved in the program. Women feel empowered when they see their efforts publicized. By openly promoting your program, you will bring the subject of women's giving out into the open and not only catch the attention of women but also get your board, staff, and community thinking about women's role in philanthropy as well.

15. *Continue to test, evaluate, and change as necessary.* Here again we can take a lesson from industry. Often when marketers introduce a new product—and that is really what development officers are doing when they launch a women's program—they continue to test it on the market to be sure that it is succeeding. If it does not sell, they change it. That is what must be done with any program that you establish. Ask questions, see what works and what does not, and make changes when necessary. For example, perhaps the women affiliated with your organization do not want to help raise money right away; maybe they need more time to learn how. Per-

haps they want first to see some programs developed within the organization that appeal to women's interests. Or they may initially think that they do not want a separate women's group and later change their minds. Whatever it is, be sure that the women are the ones creating the program and that they understand that it is flexible and can be changed to suit their needs.

You will also want to monitor your actual donation dollars and numbers to gauge the results of your program. If women are not giving more, despite being placed in leadership positions and trained in fundraising, look at what is still missing or what needs to be done differently to bring about positive and measurable results.

16. *Include objectives and strategies in all plans and efforts.* You can tell how committed an organization is to a program by looking at its operating or long-range plans. A program for women and philanthropy must be included with other responsibilities in time lines for accomplishing goals. It would not be unreasonable to make a program like this a three-year effort, with the first year devoted to developing a plan, the second to conducting focus groups and evaluating the results, and the third to setting up special committees or councils as the women have indicated.

Preparing for the Future

By developing such a plan, you will be preparing for the increasing numbers of women philanthropists, like the ones profiled in Chapter Three, as well as future generations of women who will surely see philanthropy as a way to express their values and influence the future. The success of our nation's institutions and its people may rest on the ways in which women understand their capacity to create change through their giving. Fundraisers from nonprofits large and small can play a major role in making sure that that happens.

Chapter Nine

Training Women Volunteers to Seek Major Gifts

The last decade of the twentieth century will witness a dynamic role in society for women's philanthropy. Traditional or hierarchical operating procedures within development programs may need to be altered, however, to attract and retain women as significant players in charitable institutions. Because the staff's role is often limited in time and influence, one of the most effective ways to raise funds is to train volunteers to solicit more volunteers, as well as major gifts. Philanthropist Helen Hunt, in a speech given at a conference on women's philanthropy at Harvard in 1992, revealed another solid reason for training women volunteers: "I always prefer to be asked for a gift by a woman."

Training women volunteers to solicit major gifts is essential in capital campaigns and key for ongoing development efforts. Training programs vary from organization to organization, but many common elements do exist. These elements are a systematic process, timetables, and a measurable impact. In this chapter we focus on a specific training program and timetable that were developed at the University of Wisconsin, Madison, but most of the elements of this model should prove useful to other institutions and organizations.

The timetable and plan were developed at the UW Foundation for the Council on Women's Giving of the Bascom Hill Society. We developed the training program with Alma Baron, a UW Extension professor of business, and we also consulted with other organizations and institutions around the country. The program has subsequently been applied to other institutions.

The timetable for this model is three years. During the first year, prospective donor solicitors are identified, and cultivation events are held to train them. By the end of the year, the volunteer committee should be identified and recruitment begun.

At the beginning of the second year, an initial half-day training session can take place, followed by four monthly sessions. Volunteer committee members who have made their own financial commitments and participated in the training program can then select their prospects. Some of the volunteers can begin their first contacts by the third quarter of the second year.

Committee members continue their contacts in the third year, and cultivation events should be held to involve prospects in the organization's programs. Follow-up calls by staff and committee may go on into the third year. At this time, a new class of solicitors can be recruited and the process begun afresh.

If you do not have three years for training, you may need to develop a project description at the beginning of the first training session. You should do sufficient recruitment and selling of your organization before the session so that you can devote the entire period to the solicitation itself. If you must carry out an entire training process in one daylong session, set aside the whole morning for training and the afternoon for the needs and opportunities of the charity. You will still find, however, that follow-up meetings are essential to your success.

Training volunteers for solicitation can be useful even if the organization is not mounting a capital campaign. A midwestern YWCA organized a series of three meetings to train its board and committee members in the belief that its female board would make good volunteer solicitors if acquainted with the development process.

Some of the members expressed fear about conducting a personal solicitation. However, the three training sessions helped the group become more aware of the process and ready to volunteer when actually asked to solicit. The women's fears were dispelled through knowledge and understanding.

The YWCA development director took the long view and was committed to scheduling any necessary extra time to present the total training process. The program was so successful that the director now conducts sessions for all new board members.

Creating an Environment and Recruiting Volunteers: Establishing a Committee

Before volunteers can be trained, they must be motivated to learn and do the task at hand. The first step of the process is creating an environment where the women can shape their individual understanding of the significance of their philanthropy. They have to be able to see how their personal values and concerns for society can be expressed through their gift to your organization.

In coeducational institutions and organizations, women who participate in special female committees and training programs must also be invited to join in on the coed committees, although they may certainly choose not to. However, it is best to restrict the training sessions for the women's group to women only because this provides an opportunity to involve them in a setting where they are comfortable and hence more likely to participate.

Recruiting the committee may involve one-on-one meetings between the women and key leaders or staff persons before a letter is sent with a formal invitation. Identifying and recruiting the committee may take as long as the solicitation period, and one or more events with potential committee members may be involved.

During the first year of the program at UW, cultivation events were held to involve potential prospects and committee members. To set the tone for these activities and connect the message to women specifically, the national chair, Jean Manchester-Biddick, opened each event with her own story of what had motivated her to establish the Center for Family Excellence at the School of Family Resources and Consumer Sciences at UW Madison. Manchester was widowed when the youngest of her four children was an infant, about twenty years ago. With no formal business training, she took over the family meat-purveying business and guided it to success. But as a single parent, she found it very difficult to get information on child rearing and development. She helped establish the center in the hope of promoting research and dissemination of knowledge in family studies to help today's parents.

Manchester also explained why she chose to give the lead gift to establish the Center for Women and Philanthropy. Her personal stories demonstrated her satisfaction with her ability to help improve society through giving.

At cultivation events, the philosophy of your program must be made clear through a modified focus or discussion group format, allowing the women to lead themselves to their own conclusions about why their participation and support are needed. A useful format is to hold a luncheon for prospective volunteers. Each table constitutes a discussion group that addresses five questions. A facilitator from each table reports the conclusions of the discussion to the entire group following the meal. The questions used at these events could be similar to those discussed earlier for researching female donors:

- What are the major challenges and problems facing our society?
- How does your institution or organization address these challenges and problems?
- What values would you like passed on to the next generation?
- How can you communicate these values through your institution?
- If you had $1 million to establish a permanent endowment

fund today and you could designate one project within the institution, what would that project be?

The facilitator at each table must be alert to the responses of the women, and all who attend the event should remain a part of the prospect base, even if they do not respond enthusiastically or openly to the message. The women who respond and understand the process at your event are the ones who will be good committee members and volunteers. A series of luncheons for many different prospects is a good plan for involving new women, although a limited attendance is suggested, fifty being a good number.

At several of the UW sessions, a lively presentation by a faculty member followed the focus group discussions to illustrate how women could solve social problems or perpetuate their values through a major research or outreach grant. For one event, the council invited philanthropic historian Joan M. Fisher, who gave an impassioned speech about the needs of society from a current and historical perspective and explained why it is crucial that women be philanthropists.

The setting for the training sessions should always be appropriate for the group. For national organizations such as colleges and universities, with volunteers coming from around the nation, a one-day volunteer training session should take place on the college grounds. The president's home or a local country club may be suitable for some organizations, a nice hotel room for others. A good location too is the home of one of the lead volunteers.

Staff members and volunteer committee cochairs can make follow-up calls on the women who react enthusiastically to the focus groups. The cochairs can invite them to participate as facilitators or other leaders in the training sessions to follow. A formal letter of invitation should be sent to the prospective participants, giving the dates of each session. A reply form is also enclosed, but it is not necessary that prospects indicate a definite commitment to serve on the committee. At UW, the committee members must have made a gift of $10,000 or more, or be considered a prospect at that level, to be eligible to serve on a committee. For the first training series at UW, half the council's invited list participated: the goal was to get fifteen women involved, and twenty-eight signed up.

The Formal Training Process

Six elements must be addressed during a comprehensive major gift training program for women:

1. The motivations for giving and the basic concept that major gifts come from personal, face-to-face contacts
2. The differences between men's and women's attitudes toward philanthropy and how a solicitation call may differ according to gender
3. Details of the solicitation call itself, listening skills and props to aid in making the first call, the steps of the fundraising process from cultivation to close, and how to overcome objections
4. Types of giving, including planned giving
5. The projects and needs of the organization or institution, including the details of management and finances
6. Personal examples of giving, including testimonials and presentations by the donors or by volunteers or staff members working with the donors

Whatever the time schedule or format, these elements must be emphasized. At each meeting, following the initial training sessions, they should be repeated to reinforce the educational process. The recommended number at the training session is twenty-five to allow for group discussion and personal interaction.

Session One: Half Day

This first session is the most crucial to the success of volunteer education. A half-day session may initially seem too long, but you will find that at least that much time is necessary for covering the topics, and a half day also allows a sense of camaraderie to develop among the participants. In this format, the needs of the organization are mentioned only in the introductory comments, and the remaining time is spent on training in the solicitation process and discussing motivation.

As with all educational workshops, the instructor is key to the success of the session. Her status as a volunteer or professional is not as important as her experience in public speaking and her ability to draw the audience into the learning process. Another key to success is a trained female facilitator to lead the volunteer sessions. An outside expert is well worth the expense because she will usually have more credibility in training than an individual or staff member who is known to the volunteers. A volunteer's manual should be distributed at the first session, and additional material introduced at subsequent meetings or sessions. Binders divided into sections and stamped with the logo of the organization work very well. The following topics should be covered: motivations for giving, gender differences, listening skills, asking skills, and overcoming objections. There should also be time for role playing and wrap-up.

Motivations for Giving. The facilitator should lead off the session with an overview of the day's schedule and the goals to be accomplished. She should emphasize that questions and comments are encouraged throughout the morning and stress that the session is a workshop, not a presentation.

To begin the discussion, participants should review with the facilitator a list of possible philanthropic motivations and decide whether each is more likely to motivate men or women to give. For each identified as a male motive, ask how women would express them differently. Here are some motivations cited in Kotler and Andreasen's *Strategic Marketing for Nonprofit Organizations* (1991):

- Need for self-esteem
- Need for recognition from others
- Fear of contracting the problem
- Habit or tradition
- Giving to get rid of a nuisance solicitor
- Feeling of being required to give
- Feeling of being "trapped" into giving
- Desire to give because a certain person asked
- Concern for humanity

Gender Differences. The next part of the training session should begin with a discussion of gender differences, which begin at birth (the first question asked about a new baby is invariably "Is it a girl or a boy?"), proceed through socialization (in the games that little girls and boys play), and are perpetuated by the media, especially on television and in advertising.

The topic of gender differences in communications can be introduced with a personal story by the facilitator. The story should be told in the first person, even if it is not a true story but rather one invented for purposes of the workshop.

For example, a facilitator can tell a story about riding in the car with her husband when they got lost. Guess which partner wanted to stop to ask directions? Another could be about telling a male friend or her husband that she had a backache. The man gave her advice about how to lift heavy objects safely when what she really wanted was a sympathetic ear. The man wanted the conversation to end in action; for the woman, the conversation was the action.

Stories about gender communications that include humor about ourselves (research tells us women like to laugh at themselves) lead into a discussion about women's motivations for giving. For example, "If these differences occur in our everyday conversations and lives, is it surprising that there are motivational differences between men and women in their giving? Let's discuss these differences."

Contrasts between male and female attitudes and approaches to giving should be the next topic. The facilitator must have an outline of the points to be made in order to ask leading questions, in case the participants do not bring them all out. The facilitator should write the points the audience makes on a flip chart, and depending on the group, she can end the discussion by bringing out her own list on a separate chart, presented as the conclusions of other women around the country in similar group sessions. Having given these workshops to groups of women around the nation, we can unequivocally state that any group of women will come to the same conclusions.

Participants will no doubt mention that gifts in honor or in memory of another person will be a common way for women to give. Discussion of this topic should center around women who believe that their husbands earned the money and hence that it should be directed to the husband's interest. Male institutions have received billions of dollars from women giving in memory of a dead spouse. The new movement of women and philanthropy accepts that this will continue to be the only way many women will consent to give, and we must acknowledge these women's feelings. However, we are working to overcome this old motivation, which does not encourage women to give in their own names or to support the causes they care about most profoundly. All new volunteer training programs should include mention of alternatives to giving in honor of another person. An enlightened philanthropist will give from her own heart to the areas of her own concern. She may balance her gift between her husband's interests and her own (especially if the husband is deceased), but a woman who gives in memory of her husband out of a sense of obligation will not make a good volunteer solicitor. Women who know and value themselves are the ones who will become major givers and good volunteers.

Listening Skills. The listening skills section of the workshop is important because it presents the essence of the major gift call: listening for knowledge about how the donor will connect or relate to the cause. During a large campaign, with many varied projects, solicitors should be listening for cues as to which project or projects might be of interest to the prospective donor.

The discussion of good listening also introduces the importance of the development of rapport with the prospect. A male fundraiser from a Protestant church says that he discusses the relationship of the donor to all other people in the world and then listens as she tells her own story. Philanthropy is pursued only when the prospect has a mature attitude about herself and acknowledges her uniqueness and importance in the world. The volunteer caller needs to listen to the prospect to find out how she views her own role as a world citizen.

Ask your audience for some specific bad listening habits. These will almost certainly be cited:

- *Not paying attention.* Science tells us that people think four times faster than they talk. When listening, do you use this excess time to turn your thoughts elsewhere while keeping general track of what the other person is saying?
- *Falling for buzzwords.* Do certain words, phrases, or ideas so prejudice you against the speaker that you cannot listen objectively to what is being said?

- *Not asking questions*. When puzzled or annoyed by what some-one says, do you try to get the questions straightened out immediately, or do you figure that you can straighten it out later?

- *Letting first impressions interfere*. Do you assume by a person's appearance and delivery that she will not have anything worthwhile to say?

Now ask the participants to discuss why we need to listen more. Ask them to list some of the values of good listening. Here are some that you can add to the ones they suggest:

- *Listening reduces tension*. Giving the other person a chance to get her problem or viewpoint off her chest may help clear the air of tension and hostility.

- *Listening enhances learning*. You can learn about the subject being discussed or about the person speaking if you (1) listen past words to meaning, (2) listen for the facts behind the words, (3) listen for answers to the questions you ask, (4) listen to the context of what is being said, and (5) listen to the person who is speaking (consider her emotions, intelligence, temperament, skill with words, reaction habits).

- *Listening alone may help solve a problem*. Giving a person a chance to talk through her problem may (1) clarify her think-ing about the subject and (2) provide the necessary emotional release.

- *Listening can stimulate the speaker*. Eager, alert, active listening helps the speaker do a better job of presenting her ideas.

Solicitation Visit.   After the discussion of communication skills, the facilitator should move to an example of a classic solicitation visit. The audience is asked to use what they have learned about female socialization and communication and listening skills to create a strategy to stimulate women's special motivations. How would the scenario be different if both solicitor and prospect were female? What different kinds of steps should be taken?

The group should make the following points:

- The solicitor needs to spend time getting to know the prospect. This may mean bringing her to an event or visiting her once or twice before a gift is solicited. The solicitor should relate to the prospect on a personal level, using the techniques of good communication. These techniques come naturally to most women and include "rapport talk," which involves repeating what the person has said or returning à similar comment from personal experience.

- Several of the participants may mention that they have been ignored by a fundraiser who was soliciting them with their husbands. The verbal and nonverbal attention of the fundraiser was directed exclusively at the husband. This should be addressed, with discussion of how important it is to give both partners respect and attention.

Other related concerns should also be addressed, including how to acknowledge joint gifts, as well as the following:

- Solicitors should listen closely to what the women say about their own experiences. It may be difficult for some to open up about this because they are unaccustomed to discussing how their giving relates to their values and experience. The solicitor should empathize with the donor.

- A great deal of discussion will center around the emotional state vital to a philanthropist or major giver. She must be a mature human being who values and accepts herself and the decisions that she has made. Sometimes a discussion with an older woman will begin with a story about the husband's life and her life with him. But the key with older, less self-confident women is getting them to talk about their own lives and what they have accomplished. Once the connection is made, the donor will realize that her philanthropy is a reflection of her life and values. For homemakers who believe that their worth is questionable in the eyes of modern society, the message about women and philanthropy can be immensely empowering. It can lead them to realize that their lives and values are important and can be passed on to the next generation. Fundraisers and other volunteers who affirm women's values release a powerful message and often completely revitalize the donor.

- For the career woman, this message affirms the values that she has worked for in her career or perhaps has had to hide in an unsympathetic business environment. Through philanthropy, she can demonstrate that her concerns are valid and worthwhile. Development directors are often taken aback by the enthusiastic response of career women to interest areas completely outside their professional scope.

The volunteer may feel that the majority of her visit is spent validating and reassuring the self-worth of the woman prospect—quite contrary to a visit with a man. The female prospect may, however, believe that society belittles and misunderstands the attitudes and priorities of women; thus the volunteer's support and sympathy will come as a pleasant surprise.

According to Nashville communication consultant Ruth Sweet (information conveyed in a personal communication), volunteer solicitors should be briefed on the following priorities for solicitation calls:

- The project should be related to the prospect or donor personally, and the cause or needs of the organization must be presented in the context of the woman's values.

- The female prospect should be given the opportunity to join with other women, or her friends, to support the project. Do not use peer pressure, and avoid aggressive approaches like "Jane is giving this amount. Can you?" Instead try "Jane, May, and Susan are helping us with this project. Can we count on your help too?"

- The "close" or "ask" will be the beginning of further involvement for the donor. If the volunteer is not involved in the actual ask (some women want to avoid any talk of money), she can be included in the cultivation and stewardship stages with a staff member who makes the ask. Another approach, which was used in the Wellesley campaign, involves a letter sent in addition to the visit, stating the amount of money hoped for from the prospect.

At this time, it would be a good idea to mention that a solicitation call is not like going to lunch with a complete stranger and then asking them for half a million dollars over dessert. It is more like a courtship requiring several "dates" before asking for a commitment. Because most women have never been solicited before for a major gift, and because women generally like to become more involved with a project before giving money, the caller may need to make as many as six visits before closing. This fact is surprising to many first-time volunteers, both male and female. You can point out that major gift solicitation is a much different volunteer process from selling tickets to a dance or a basketball game or soliciting for the annual church drive.

Asking Skills. Next offer an example of a typical volunteer fundraising call, and ask the group to react. You might make up an example in which the volunteer begins talking about the cause or organization, does not tell what the meeting is about, and ignores signals given by the prospect. Make the caller and the prospect male. Ask the group for reactions to the call.

At this point, participants can review the basics of good volunteer asking skills, and the facilitator should be prepared to make any points the audience misses. The following points should be covered:

- *Planning.* Volunteer solicitation involves research, getting the appointment, and preparing for the contact. (A sample prospect visit planner is presented in Exhibit 9.1.)
- *Establishing trust.* The solicitor must establish credibility, make believable claims, demonstrate competence and a problem-solving attitude, listen attentively, and demonstrate empathy.
- *Qualifying needs.* Before the call, the volunteer should work with development staff to determine questions to ask, word questions properly, and prepare to listen.
- *Providing customized solutions.* During the call, the solicitor should summarize occasionally for clarity, handle objections positively and respectfully, stress the value of the organization and this interaction, dramatize enthusiastically, and generate action.
- *Building partnerships.* This involves written communications, follow-up activities, and record keeping. (A sample follow-up report appears in Exhibit 9.2.)

Donor Stages. Alma Baron explains that there are specific stages a donor goes through, in which she asks herself certain questions. These stages need to be discussed with the group. As in other dialogues, the facilitator or leader should try to get the audience to come up with the answers but be prepared to help them. The stages are trust (Do I like this person?), need (How badly do I want this problem to be solved?), help (Can this person or institution help

Exhibit 9.1. Prospect Visit Planner.

Name: _____

Address: _____   City: _____

State: _____   ZIP: _____   Phone: _____

Key Contact: _____

Current Situation:
Objective(s) of visit:
Benefit of objective to prospect:
University program(s) to discuss:
☐ Features   ☐ Benefits
Main issues from last contact:
Other charitable interests:
Questions to Uncover or Clarify Needs:
☐ Anticipated objections   ☐ Responses
Information to gather for next call or step:
Action Step: ☐ What commitment will I ask this prospect to make?

Exhibit 9.2. Follow-Up Report.

Name: _____

Objective(s) from Volunteer:

Decision Reached:

Summary of Call:

☐ New Information   ☐ General information

☐ Financial information or projections

New needs	Opportunity	Priority

Action plans

Interpersonal information	Philosophy

Self-Evaluation:

☐ What did I do well?   ☐ What can I improve on?

me and the people I care about?), and decision anxiety (Should I actually do this?). (This information was conveyed to the authors in a personal communication.) Volunteers who understand these stages can listen for them during the call and are better able to react as they come up. Following are some suggestions as to how the volunteer can handle each stage.

1. Trust

- *Be prepared.* Think ahead of time about what you bring to the relationship and how to increase your understanding of the prospect's point of view.

- *Make a good first impression.* Establish common ground, be competent in your knowledge of the institution, and communicate honestly your intention for the call.

- *Adjust your attitude.* Your attitude should reflect your ability and desire to solve a problem. Set your sights high; people behave as you expect them to behave. Have a relaxed, confident style so as not to increase the individual's initial stress.

- *If you don't know, ask.* Ask permission to ask questions. Have a written list of questions prepared before the call, and do not be afraid to take notes.

2. Need

- *Listen actively.* Prepare yourself to listen by clearing your mind and getting ready to expend a great deal of energy. Listen selectively for central ideas that are relevant. Reinforce those areas of relevance.

- *Summarize.* State your summary of the situation and problem to be solved, and ask for agreement.

3. Help

- *State your case.* Keep it short, and say only what is important to the person you are speaking with.

- *Back up your case.* Use testimony from others, stories, referrals. You have to believe in your cause and appeal directly to your prospect as a person. Remember, people do things for their reasons, not yours.

4. Decision Anxiety

- *Overcome objections.* An objection may come as an emotional shock. Use a creative, problem-solving approach. Objections are an indication that the person you are communicating with is interested and wants more information. Remember, though, that an objection may be a smoke screen; that is, the first objection is rarely the real objection. You do not need to resolve an objection on the spot. Rather, give a passive response, acknowledge any anger, and listen. This deflates the prospect's tension and gives you time to try to understand her feelings and thoughts. Help her clarify her concerns, and keep her talking. Once she is calmer and the real objection has surfaced, present your answer. Ask for her commitment to a new or changed position.

- *Employ closing techniques.* Be aware of the closing approach that is most comfortable for you and will minimize the individual's decision anxiety. There are three basic closing statements: asking directly for a gift; asking what she wants to support, rather than whether she wants to support a cause; and indicating that her objection is only a minor point in the whole case.

Overcoming Objections. We cannot overemphasize the important role that overcoming objections plays in training. Being turned down is the major worry of female volunteer fundraisers, and they often take it personally. Helping them identify and overcome possible objections before they even make the calls will greatly diminish their concerns. This should be tied into the listening process as they, the future volunteers, will play a key role in listening to prospects and helping overcome their objections. For practice, the facilitator can pose typical objections to the audience and ask for a response.

The organizing committee should assemble a list of objections—both common ones and those particular to women—and suggested replies before the training session. After the discussion, the list can be distributed for reference. Many of the common objections voiced by women are discussed in Chapter Five, but you will want your examples to be much more specific to your organization.

Role Playing. This part of the session concerns preparation for the first call. Volunteers should be trained in the following steps:

1. Call and write the prospect first, or set up a casual contact in a business or social setting.
2. Talk to the prospect briefly about the project and ask to meet with her to discuss it further.
3. Explain in advance why you want the meeting, avoiding vague language.
4. Set up a specific appointment.

The training committee should distribute to the audience a set of examples of various prospects and situations and pair the volunteers to play the parts of donor and solicitor. There should be at least five different case examples, with each pair receiving at least two examples. Background information about the fictitious prospect should be included in each example, and the solicitor is expected to practice her listening skills and explain her duties as a volunteer fundraiser. Here are two examples that can be adapted to your situation:

Example A

The wealthy wife of a corporation president (both are alumni of the university) thinks that what her husband gives to the university is enough. How would you persuade her to give a gift in her own name?

Profile: The wife is a new older woman, born before 1945. She grew up in the secure but conformist 1950s. She now heads a community foundation but did not work outside the home until her children were grown. Her values have been affected by the Great Depression. She sees herself as a role model. In fact, she has always "gotten along" in a man's world by compromising. She says that she influences her husband's decisions. Her own interests are fairly well defined. She is very much involved with her children and grandchildren.

Example B

A young woman supporter of your organization has just completed a nasty battle with her brothers to gain control of the closely held family corporation following their father's death. She is actively involved in the management of the company. How would you involve her with your organization and interest her in making a large donation?

Profile: This prospect is a baby boomer, born between 1945 and 1960. Her husband also works for the family business, and they have one small child. She manages her own finances, as well as those of the corporation. She has been on the board of Planned Parenthood and the city planning commission.

Wrap-Up. The final part of the half-day session is spent in a quick review and summary of the basic steps of a call, along with any final comments by the volunteer chairs or staff. Now it is up to the volunteer chairs to define clearly the next step for the committee to take.

The cochairs should point out at this time that the goal is for each woman volunteer to make three to five personal solicitation visits over the next year. They should explain that although each person has her own individual style of soliciting or involving someone in a charity, the purpose remains for all volunteers to complete the training session and then work with their committee chairs to determine how they can most comfortably participate in the campaign. Remember that the invitation initially sent to the women asking them to serve on the committee and attend the training session did not require any commitment or define the role that a participant might eventually play. In other words, by attending the training session, the participants have not agreed to make five calls. Women who did attend the training sessions, however, should be making their own contributions at a certain level and will likely be willing to participate in some volunteer capacity to help the annual drive campaign.

What you must do in your training session is create a level of comfort in the major gift-giving process. By the end of the first half-day session, volunteers should know that they can be very helpful and influential in the introduction and cultivation stages, as they usually present the case much more convincingly than a paid professional.

The ask and closing stages, in contrast, can be the most alarming and therefore the most uncomfortable parts of the solicitation process. Trainers can show that the major gift process is divided into several stages and assure volunteers that if they can make a general ask, a staff person can then close the gift. For instance, during a second visit, the volunteer could say, "Jane, you can express your interest in the children's arts by making this project possible. We hope you will consider becoming a benefactor to this project. I would like to introduce you to the development director, who can talk to you more about it." The development director can then give the specifics of the program and ask Jane, "Would you consider a gift of $100,000 to this project?"

Session Two: Role Playing and Assignment of Names

The second training session can be held over a two-hour period, one month after the first. This workshop will focus on reviewing the major gift process while working more on the specifics of a call. This meeting will also introduce the details of a specific project and related giving opportunities at the organization or institution.

A good beginning for the second session is to have a female division head in a social service agency tell how the program has helped her clients. Research and experience have shown that women want more accountability and details about the projects that they wish to fund.

"Women want the big picture and all the details to fill in that big picture. They want to see the specifics," says Pleasant Rowland, president of Pleasant Company (personal communication). She describes the early stages of test marketing for her company, which sells high-quality dolls and accessories. "When I explained my concept to a test group, their reaction to the product was negative. Then we brought out the product and showed them in detail what the product line would be. They liked the wholeness of the product—from book to doll to doll's clothes and girls' clothes."

"As the president of my own foundation," Rowland adds, "I find that many of the proposals I receive lack the details I need to relate to the project. In the same way, universities fail to gain women's attention by not giving out the specifics of the project up front."

A primary purpose of the training sessions is to provide information that the volunteers can use in their solicitations, but another function is to contribute to their own enlightenment so that they become good donors in their own right.

Session two consists of two elements: role playing and assignment of prospect names.

Role Playing. Education through role playing has been offered in major-gift training sessions for males and females across the nation. However, Marjorie Tobias, volunteer cochair of the University of Wisconsin Women's Council, sees special value in role playing with a group of women volunteers. "In this all-female context, you can create a sense of collegiality among the committee through role playing. One of the most successful formats is to have a humorous 'wrong' call to ease the audience and set the tone. At the UW's Women's Council, we chose to go further into the area of the psychology of women laughing at themselves" (conveyed in a personal communication). In this case, the two cochairs and staff person dressed in silly costumes and made up a funny routine breaking every rule in the book.

Cochair Katherine S. Nordeen reported, "Some of the humor was that the 'wrong' call involved many aspects that the women were familiar with because they had experienced them firsthand. The primary error is that the solicitors don't ask what the person's interests are—they try to push their own project to the prospect. The prospect gives clues about her own interest but is ignored by the solicitors. We had even more fun by billing the role players in the agenda as 'mystery guests'" (personal communication).

The next twenty minutes of the presentation should feature three members of the committee playing the roles of prospect, volunteer, and staffer on a good call. These three players, who have been asked by the cochairs to make the presentation, should meet prior to the session to discuss their dialogue, based on what they learned in the first training session. They should listen to the prospect and review the case well. The audience then critiques each of the calls.

Assignment of Names. Pairing the volunteer solicitor to the right prospects is a major task and requires a great deal of attention. Preparing the list of prospects is a separate function from volunteer training, but the two are often accomplished by the same method of identification. Prospect rating, however, is completely separate and needs to be completed before the training sessions begin. At the training session, you should have a complete list of potential prospects in hand for the volunteers to review.

The ideal number for a rating session is six volunteers: this number will allow the participants to tell all they know about the prospects. If the group gets too large, very few will openly share their information. Older women who know everyone in the community are excellent to serve on rating committees, as well as senior women who feel that they have completed their leadership roles in the community yet want to help. As with the solicitation committee, it is essential that the raters be major donors to your organization. You may ask a few women who are financial or legal professionals to serve on the rating committee, but these women should also be at least nominal donors. You must have accurate information about your prospects and present the lists in a professional manner, giving name and capacity rating. Some organizations also add an interest, or inclination, indicator. Realize that women have the same reaction as men to ratings—they understand the necessity of them but are uncomfortable with categorizing people. Your organizers must nevertheless use the ratings and display a completely relaxed attitude toward them.

At the second training session, an entire discussion must focus on the name assignments. One format is to ask the volunteer chairs to meet with teams separately, no more than six to a team. During these meetings, the list of prospects is reviewed, and the volunteer fundraisers are asked to identify whom they would choose as their contacts. Terminology here is very important. Stress that the individuals they choose will be considered not just prospects but contacts and friends. Be sure to use the word *contact* rather than *prospect*. The object is to work with the contact to develop a relationship with the charity, not just seek money. The money will come if the relationship has been established.

In the case of a nursing home, for example, the development director asked her volunteers to invite other women in to see the facility and meet with the director. In many cases, the volunteers may want to give a personal tour without involving the director, if they feel that their contacts are not yet ready for a direct meeting.

A team of women volunteers who choose their contacts

together may pair up to make the calls. Women enjoy the friendship and contact with peers and prefer making calls with acquaintances. Two volunteers or a staff member and a volunteer make good combinations for calls on both males and females. Women will also choose primarily other women as their contacts, though some may select couples or single men.

A team leader will serve as a resource for the other members. It is difficult for any staff person to handle more than twenty volunteers, especially novices. Team leaders can keep in touch with the volunteers and funnel information to the staff. They can also help by making joint calls with the members if they wish.

The training committee should receive the list of prospects before the second training session and should return it after the volunteers have chosen their contacts, with the selections marked off and any other names they wish to contact added. Again, allow for flexibility in the process, and if some participants do not care to make individual calls themselves, ask if they would accompany another participant or a staff member to share their experiences with a contact. Allow a maximum of one month for the volunteers to select their contacts, meet with them, and report to the training committee.

At each subsequent meeting, the lists of contacts and volunteers assigned to each participant should be available. The leaders will need to make many follow-up calls to their volunteers and may want to hold several team meetings.

Session Three: Project Description, Fund Management, and Testimonials

The third session, held one month after the second, focuses on the institution's specific needs, the administration and management of funds, and testimonials. The list of contact sign-ups is again distributed for verification.

Like the previous session, this one continues to focus on a specific project of the institution and allows the women to meet and discuss the details with the staff members involved. A twenty-minute presentation will give the women good insight into an individual project.

An overview of the institution's financial basis is crucial at this third meeting, and detailed financial reports should be distributed for reference. It is important to divulge and discuss how money received by the institution is managed, and a presentation by a female financial officer would be appropriate. If you are raising money for endowments, you need a circular explaining the endowment structure, the minimum requirements, and all relevant details concerning gifts received.

Testimonials by current donors are a most powerful tool, and by the third meeting the group should have reached the point where the members feel comfortable with one another. Having leaders talk about their own gifts and why they gave them is very effective. Your key leaders will set the tone, and a strong presentation of their motivations can be moving and inspiring. The women will speak from the heart about their lives and values. Sharing experiences is great for motivation; in this case, the women will learn how others have experienced philanthropy. This process could include descriptions of the specific projects the women are funding and reasons why the women deemed them worthy of their support.

Session Four: Short Course in Planned Giving

The fourth session is a ninety-minute presentation by a planned-giving expert who reviews all of the major planned-giving vehicles and tax ramifications. This discussion could be incorporated into the general training period, but a longer session devoted to the subject is helpful. At this session, the volunteers will learn of giving vehicles that they themselves might also find useful.

Session Five and Monthly Meetings Thereafter

If you are in the position of training your volunteers for a specific campaign within a specific time period, you will want to meet with them monthly while they are working. If your training is planned over a longer time frame, bimonthly meetings may be more appropriate. But at least in the initial stages, monthly meetings are preferable.

The following elements should be incorporated into each meeting:

- An update on the progress of the volunteer fundraisers, including successes and setbacks
- Reports on specific projects within the institution by individuals directly involved, such as students, grant recipients, program staff, artists, or curators
- Reports and testimonials about the donors the volunteers have met and their reasons for giving

Cultivation Events

It is essential that you periodically stage cultivation events to which your volunteer fundraisers can invite prospects. A campaign kickoff is one such event—with a definite additional sell. Two events per year could be planned to help inform potential major contributors about the institution, involve future major donors, and maintain contact with your current supporters. For example, an environmental group could hold an annual summer breakfast meeting on a restored prairie. Even if held only once a year, a cultivation event can help your solicitors.

Cultivation events are not fundraisers, as many novices believe. In the major gift business, you do not invite your prospects to an event and charge them more than a nominal amount. If you do, prospects get the impression that they have already made a contribution by purchasing event tickets. Nor should your major cultivation event be open to the general public; only major donors and major gift prospects should be invited. Attendance at such an event should be limited to no more than sixty people.

A luncheon for ten carefully selected people also makes an excellent major gift cultivation event. At large universities and other organizations that define major gifts as $100,000 or more, a cultivation event can be a dinner for a small group with the chancellor or a lecture for a group of forty individuals.

Social service agencies without the funds or the right environment for cultivation events can invite prospects to the home of the director or a major donor. This format was used by the YWCA, which made it clear to the prospects that the meeting was not a fundraising event but rather a get-acquainted session for community leaders and outstanding women. It was explained that the purpose of the gathering was to interest the participants in becoming involved in the YWCA at a future time.

Another idea is to offer a "target seminar" on the project in need of funding, followed by a luncheon with a speaker on a broad topic related to women as philanthropists. Events of this kind that involve prospects personally will assist your women volunteers in developing ties between their prospects and the charity.

Note that cultivation events should be presented to the committee as a small part of the major gift process. If you dwell on events too much, they will take on too much importance, and the committee will view them as the end-all. The committee may be consulted regarding ideas for the events, but it is best to leave the planning to the staff. Emphasize to the committee members that their job is to get the prospects to attend.

Successful Fundraising: Investing in Volunteers

The definition of success in fundraising is evolving. Whereas we once measured success by simply counting up the dollars received, now we ask if we have established a better relationship with the prospect. Some calls might not result in immediate gifts, but they help identify people to involve in the organization, to serve on its boards, and to approach in the future for major gifts. Furthermore, it is rare to receive a major gift from an individual who has not had some prior relationship with the organization. The process points to the importance of rating your major gift prospects by their capacity to give and making sure that you visit all of the top-rated prospects.

This long-term fundraising philosophy is clear to women, who recognize that relationships take years to nurture. Indeed, your training program is really the process of building and nurturing friendships and relationships. Understand that you are making an investment in your volunteers through the training process, and you must value them as a part of the institution. In training volunteers to raise funds for your current project, you are giving them the insight to become key players for your organization for years to come.

A training program for women may take longer than one for men. Not only are most women unfamiliar with the process, but they want to be extremely well prepared when they do their work. Women are particularly concerned about knowing all the details. In the long run, they can be the very best of advocates for an institution because they truly feel like part of the institutional family. Further, the staff will likely learn a great deal more in the sessions than the women volunteers. Even for seasoned professionals, the personal values and true philanthropic spirit that the women bring to these gatherings give new vitality to the word *philanthropy*. Best of all, the women want to enjoy their work with your organization, and you will enjoy working with them.

In her speech at Harvard philanthropist Helen Hunt said, "Women want an active role whenever we give, and special care needs to be given to that concern. I can't stress that enough. We want our intellectual contributions as well as our checks acknowledged." She referred to herself as a fundraiser and said, "Fundraising is so much fun once you get started. Helping other women raise money is so very gratifying."

Chapter Ten

Reinventing the Capital Campaign

If women are to give major gifts to our institutions to the extent to which they are capable, a new capital campaign must be designed. Capital campaigns are being mounted these days in organizations and institutions of every size, but they invariably follow the male model, as conceived by Harold "Si" Seymour. This prototype worked well for years because the majority of gifts were given and sought by men. The first few pages of Seymour's book, *Designs for Fundraising* (1988), exemplify the differences between men's motivations for giving and what our research indicates about women's. For example, one of the basic motivations that Seymour describes is a responsible concern for continuity. Our research has substantially demonstrated that women are not motivated to preserve the status quo but rather to bring about change. Not once in the past six years have we heard a woman mention that her gift was prompted by a desire to perpetuate an institution.

Although many of Seymour's theories are still valid and useful, it is clear that his book was written for campaigns appealing to men. Even his rating sheets assume that all prospects are male, and he advises recruiting "men of standing" to lead the campaigns. In the list of guidelines he wrote to help fundraisers understand how to ask for gifts, most apply exclusively to men: for example, presenting winning ideas, not needy causes; striving for measurable and praiseworthy attainment; relishing earned reward and recognition; and going with the winning horse—all have a strictly male appeal.

We are not deprecating these theories, which have proved successful in an appropriate setting, but times have changed since 1966, when Seymour's book was first published. Women are as much a resource as men and must be included in our present-day fundraising efforts. The campaigns that lead to future successes will be those that take note of the differences between men's and women's aspirations.

Douglas Lawson's book *Give to Live* (1991) more accurately describes today's complex motives for giving and sharing. He recognizes psychological influences, how we are asked, and our early training—the very things that inspire women to give. He also connects the head to the heart, explaining that by helping others, we can receive just as much, and shows that generosity makes the world a better place. Lawson also discusses the need for change and for making a difference; again, these are major reasons why women choose to give money.

What follows in this chapter are the principles for the campaign of the future. This is not to be read like a recipe; our population is too diverse for that. The campaign we outline draws on what we have learned from books like *Give to Live* and from campaigns that have been successful in women's colleges and organizations. It reflects the new corporate structures, which emphasize small teams, change, and reinvention. It is based on the experiences of fundraisers who are not afraid of experimentation. Our campaign esteems the human imagination and includes men and women in the same ratios as they are represented in our institutions and organizations.

While designing our campaign, we kept three important concepts in mind:

- Campaigns are about people, not about buildings or endowments. They are about people caring, people asking, and people giving. The most successful capital campaigns will be those that involve the most people at all levels and phases.

- Campaigns are about relationships. They are about developing and maintaining connections between our institutions and their constituencies.

- Campaigns are about communicating and listening to what people say. They are about understanding and assimilating messages and knowing whom we are talking to and why. Our messages must be relevant, persuasive, and imaginative.

Before Launching the Campaign

Be prepared to create a flexible campaign that is personalized to your cause and the people involved. There is no one right way to conduct a campaign, but there is a wrong way. Not only should women be major players in any modern campaign, but diversity of all kinds should be encouraged.

Today's campaigns will be more time-consuming: flexibility takes time. Successful campaigns will always be in flux, and we need to be continuously alert to what is working and what is not. Don't be afraid to change, try new things, or take a chance. For example, if we know that baby boomers and women like to give locally and our cause goes well beyond the community, we should look at efforts like Apple Computer's employee-giving campaign, designed by Mal Warwick & Associates of Berkeley, California. Researchers tested several ideas on the employees before coming up with the successful slogan "Think Globally. Give Locally." With this sentiment they acknowledge the local community interests of baby boomers while opening their eyes to problems beyond their front doors ("Direct Mail Helps . . . ," 1993).

"Adoption philanthropy," the idea of Boston College's Paul Schervish, links the donor directly to the receiver. It came to national attention when Eugene Lang conceived his "I have a dream" campaign to award college money to underprivileged high school graduates (Van Til, 1992). Because women want to feel a personal connection to an organization and are committed to volunteering, this concept could well be of high interest to them. Think of the potential results if this were applied to projects within our organizations. More time would be spent, yes, but it would open the possibility of greater and larger gifts.

Even within standard groups, there will be diversity. All men or all women will not behave in a certain way, as the Wellesley campaign confirmed. In a conversation with several women from coeducational institutions, Linda Welter, former assistant vice president for resources for the college, reported that alumnae who were businesswomen and those who were homemakers had very different interests.

> Some women focused on financial planning and management practices as a way to build a strong case for support while others identified with Wellesley's history, traditions, and legacy of alumnae leaders. Everyone wanted to be certain that the campaign would provide the financial resources needed to maintain the highest standards for admission and academic excellence. The campaign statement "Ever New, Ever Wellesley" combined many different perspectives into a common vision for Wellesley's future.
>
> The campaign plan was based on the very successful Harvard model designed for their $350 million drive. However, Wellesley's process was formed by her volunteers. Plans were tested, modified, and adapted to better suit various constituencies. Wellesley alumnae created their own campaign. I believe the volunteers had fun and I'd like to think they'd do it again if presented with the opportunity.

As we ask women to stretch to make their gifts, we should also stretch the boundaries in designing our campaigns. We should strive to make fundraising fun, rather than just doing things the way they have always been done.

Involvement

Have you looked at your organization or institution's image and programs from a woman's viewpoint? Have you taken an inventory of the number of women involved in leadership positions? Women are insulted when they are considered as an afterthought. Indeed, two major national educational institutions had no success attracting women to their capital campaigns until they developed a full-scale program that would include and involve women and deal with issues of interest to them. The revamped efforts will no doubt pay off in a few years, but current fundraising continues to suffer because women simply did not respond to the schools' inept last-minute appeals for money.

At least three years before your campaign gets under way, you should begin developing a relationship between the institution and its women constituents, not only so that the women will be prepared to give but also to identify the most suitable campaign leaders.

Campaign Structure

Although this chapter reinvents the inner process of the capital campaign, it retains most of the traditional framework, including campaign leadership and structure. However, you may choose to reconfigure your campaign totally. Oregon Health Sciences University in Portland, Oregon, has done just that with what they call the focused affinity strategy, "an alternative to capital campaigns." This new style came about as a result of a small staff that could not manage large numbers of volunteers. Initial focus groups were organized to raise awareness, solicit views, and obtain program commitment to the financial needs of specific university units. These units had become fairly autonomous within the institution, so an "affinity group" made up of four individuals was formed for each unit to define needs and develop a communication process and strategy with the other groups. In so doing, the volunteers truly became a part of the process and knew the case statement thoroughly.

The planning stage lasted three months to a year before the solicitation process began. At first, the volunteers were reluctant to ask for gifts, but they did set up the calls and accompany the development officer on them. Over time, the volunteers became more assertive and aware of the effect of their own personal contribution of time and money. By mid campaign, they were confidently asking the prospects to join them in supporting the institution.

The volunteers were heavily vested and involved in the campaign, and they were always looking for better ways to do things. In time, they allowed staff to take on more of a supportive role rather than a purely directive one. The first phase of the campaign raised more than its goal, and additional affinity groups were established for the next phase.

The Oregon group did point out some negatives: a campaign of this type is a time-intensive process for staff, the process is more awkward to get off the ground because volunteers want to know why everything is not in place yet, and it requires that goals be ranked by priority before fundraising begins rather than using a broader shopping-list approach. However, the university believes that these negatives are far outweighed by the benefits of having people energized through their own success, the increased commitment of established volunteers, and the continuing connection developed from the volunteers' involvement (Tanner, 1992, p. 3).

Fundraising Counsel

Many organizations, as they launch a capital campaign, hire fundraising consultants who can draw on their vast experience with the community and with similar organizations that they have assisted. If you plan to hire fundraising counsel, there are a few factors to keep in mind.

Not only are capital campaigns changing, but so are consultants. Previously, successful fundraisers tended to leave their organizations and establish their own consulting firms, most frequently in large cities. In the past five or six years, however, most towns of any size have local people who have become consultants through regional experience. To compete with the less expensive locals, some ingenious larger firms are contracting with specialty teams located outside their geographical range. These teams focus on fundraising for one particular type of organization, such as historic preservation, higher education, human services, health care, the environment, or various cultural organizations. The large contracting firm provides marketing and administrative support to the independent contractor.

We mention this because you should be aware of your options as you look at consulting firms to help in your campaign. There may be alternatives that were unheard of even a couple of years ago. Whatever you decide, when conducting interviews with top candidates, make sure that they are prepared to listen to you and your constituents. The days of flying in staff, conducting the campaign, and then flying them out is outmoded and unwise when we are trying to build lasting connections and relationships with our donors.

We recommend putting together a list of potential firms and sending them a proposal request. The request should contain brief facts about your organization and some specific questions for them to answer. You will want to include a question or two dealing with their recommendations for incorporating diversity into your campaign consulting.

Case Statement Preparation

Wellesley College called them "dialogue dinners," dinners held with alumnae and their spouses to determine the primary issues among the constituency before setting out to write the campaign statement. An overview was circulated prior to the meeting, and people were invited to discuss its content with the president. Following the meetings, questionnaires were distributed to the participants, asking about their level of interest in supporting specific issues.

This participatory and collaborative effort involved people in the campaign while it was still being conceived. As we have learned, women want to create, and this was a fine opportunity to do so. This method could easily be applied to our capital campaigns, and the dialogues and questionnaires form a basis for the case statement. Be sure to emphasize themes that all people, not just women, will be motivated by: change, making a difference, creating a better society, and diversity.

A case statement should do all of the following:

- Create a vision
- Communicate that vision
- Aim high, but not too high (women are put off by a campaign that is too large and all-encompassing; it makes them feel that their participation will be ineffectual)
- Provide specific causes to which people can give, and be sure to include women's interests (draw from what your women have been telling you in their focus groups)
- Get people excited

Test your case statement by sending it to major contributors and their spouses for reactions. Then listen to their responses and suggestions. Take their questions and concerns very seriously, and show that you value them. Women in particular aren't used to this kind of attention, and you may be surprised at the way they thank you.

Precampaign Phase

Many organizations are no longer jumping immediately into feasibility studies; now they conduct a precampaign program first. This phase focuses on an external readiness assessment while preparing the organization or institution for both the feasibility study and the campaign itself. Begin by establishing a precampaign committee made up of people (make sure that about half are women) who are currently involved with your organization or who are good prospects but may not know what the organization represents. You can use this group to test your case statement on. Use it as your sounding board. Group members can provide you with names of prospects for the feasibility study. They will also receive the first results of the study after your review.

You should seek to gain support with this first group and make advocates of them through your dialogue. Key members of the committee can be asked to set up small gatherings of four or five good leaders, prospects, and spouses in their area. At the meetings, the chief administrators of your institution can talk about the institution and ask for more input on the case statement. These meetings are like modified focus groups, with the administrator providing initial background material and leading the discussion. Meetings like this will help create awareness, establish a bond, and solidify your case statement. This phase is also valuable when doing a readiness assessment of your internal procedures and staffing.

You may wish to give these volunteers small gifts appropriate to the institution to keep them motivated and connected during a campaign. Be sure the gifts are modest and meaningful so that the institution does not appear too affluent or wasteful.

Nucleus Funding

By the time the dialogue dinners, precampaign committee meetings, and smaller meetings hosted by members are over, some money should already have been pledged. These funds will provide a nucleus for the campaign and give people confidence in its ultimate success. Board members need to be very aware at this point of their responsibility for making the campaign succeed. They will have been included in at least one of the preliminary functions, and some should by now have made a pledge or gift.

Feasibility Study

No campaign over $100,000 should proceed without a feasibility study conducted by outside counsel. It provides valuable information concerning various aspects, including whether you can raise money and, if so, how much. As with other campaign concerns, women should be included in the same ratio as they are represented in your organization or on your campus.

Only by interviewing women will you get their opinions about projects that they believe are important and would be willing to support. Feasibility studies, like focus groups, are an especially effective tool to use for this, as women are generally delighted to be asked for their opinions and will usually participate willingly. Because not everyone interviewed at this point will know what your organization or institution is doing, the feasibility study will help inform people, involve them, and connect them to you. We advise person-to-person contacts if at all possible, and letters of thanks should be sent to the participants. Everyone interviewed for a feasibility study should be asked what individual commitment he or she might make. This will get women thinking about their gift and its size, knowing that others are also being asked the same question. Of course, the feasibility study will help refine the case statement, so be sure that the campaign goal realistically reflects the financial support that people are willing to commit.

Campaign Leadership

An old Chinese proverb says, "Women hold up half the sky." Women should hold up half the campaign by serving and contributing in the same proportion as they are represented in the organization. To ensure this, the number of women to serve in the campaign cabinet and on other committees should be set early on, and this goal should be met by all appropriate means.

Balancing the leadership will be easier if there are male and female cochairs. A married couple is ideal if both are committed to the cause and taken equally seriously by the constituents and the committees. It is important to be prepared to suggest women as members. In fact, diversity of all kinds should be encouraged, as women prospects in particular will ask about this.

When asking women to serve on committees, it is also important to keep in mind their other responsibilities. The committee is going to be only one segment of their lives, and your expectations must be realistic. Men will often agree to do something and then not participate to the extent that they should, but women more frequently take the obligations seriously—all of them—and will not want to involve themselves unless they feel they can commit 100 percent. You may need to tone down your expectations when explaining their job duties. However, they will want to be reassured that they are going to be useful and have enough to do, rather than serving as just another name on a committee roster. Remember that most women have not had as much experience with this kind of work as their male counterparts and do not have their confidence. In fact, lacking experience, women may doubt their ability to contribute either their time or their money.

When recruiting a woman to be a cabinet member, it is wise to approach her accompanied by a friend of hers (male or female). A good way to begin is to make sure that the woman is included in the precampaign planning committee or the feasibility study. If this is not possible, begin by seriously asking for her advice. Even if she does not join you, you will have received some valuable information and established a relationship.

Note that a separate women's committee as part of the campaign cabinet is not usually a good idea. It conveys the impression of relegating the important tasks to the cabinet and giving the "little women" something to "keep them happy."

Recruiting Campaign Volunteers

The more people you have involved in your campaign, the more likely it is to succeed. That is why this is an appropriate time to recruit women as campaign volunteers. As you expand your base, you have a natural constituency to bring parity to your organization. This is also the time to educate your women about the power of giving—their giving as well as that of others. You can talk about philanthropy in general and about women's history of combining their sense of social responsibility with philanthropy. Also point out that it is no longer enough to donate only time; they must also donate money. A good many men can benefit from this message as well. But the difference is that once the women are signed up, they will come to the sessions. Men will often agree to serve and then not show up for any of the training sessions or even the solicitation, whereas women will usually ask many questions about their involvement before they decide but then carry through to a greater degree once they have made the commitment. A relatively easy way to ensure women's involvement is to ask the spouse or partner of each recruited male. Not all will join, but those who do give you the decided advantage of having a great team for calling on other couples.

Campaign Materials

One of the most important and most expensive components of any campaign is the literature written by campaign counsel and produced out-of-house. You must maintain control over these written materials and keep in mind the three elements of any good campaign: people, relationships, and communication. Each time the copy and photos come to you, ask yourself whether the material is honest and direct. Does it recognize the importance of people's commitment and invite them into a long-term relationship? Does it help build confidence in your organization? Is it stylish and eye-catching without being pompous or arrogant? Is it inclusive and welcoming of everyone in the campaign? Are males and females represented in numbers equal to their membership or enrollment? Are programs of particular interest to women, such as schools of nursing and education, balanced with those of interest to men? Are minority members in evidence in the materials and the programs that they will be asked to fund? Have you considered the different ways in which men and women communicate, as described in books such as Deborah Tannen's *You Just Don't Understand: Women and Men in Conversation* (1990)? Are these ideas addressed in your text and layouts? Does the text incorporate the voices of volunteer leaders?

Once you are satisfied with the initial copy and layouts, test the material. Get people's reactions before you spend money on production. This is a good time to reconvene your campaign planning committee to ask its advice again. Or, as with the case statement, send the material to generous past donors and their spouses for feedback. Heed their advice. They represent your market and know best what will have appeal.

The Campaign

The campaign kickoff, like every other get-together during the campaign, should be celebratory fun. In creating a campaign that belongs to the people, there should be kickoffs in all major geographical areas where your organization or institution is represented. If you can afford it, invite your entire membership or all alumni as guests. These events help build confidence among your constituents and heighten their awareness of the institution. The kickoffs can be spaced over a period of time, even years if necessary. But following a particular kickoff event, the campaign should then focus on that city, state, or region. Kickoffs should be in keeping with local and regional interests, combining dignity with fun.

Screening Sessions and Research

Once again, it is wise to include female prospects for screening in the same percentage as they are represented in the organization. If the woman is not herself a constituent but is married to an alumnus or member, she can be counted, but only if she is called on with her husband. This will require a commitment on the part of both the organization and the administration because research on women prospects is more difficult than research on men. Women are harder to track because most change their names when they marry. Moreover, because women still have not broken the "glass ceiling" or made it on Fortune 500 boards in representative numbers, traditional sources like Dun & Bradstreet contain few female listings. However, with record numbers of women going into law, the *Martindale Hubbell* Law Directory and other sources now maintain records on many women. Women attorneys can be most generous.

Who's Who of American Women contains biographies of more than 24,500 women who have excelled in a particular specialty area or profession. This informative guide is updated every other year. Periodicals such as *Working Woman* and *Executive Female* also profile outstanding women.

To find information about a wife without a career, you should look for material on her husband, which may include something about her, in addition to indicators of the family's financial resources and interests. For both male and female prospects and their spouses, newspaper articles are your most valuable source of material.

Once the material has been gathered, screening sessions should be held, and women should be invited to them—again, in the same proportion as they are represented in the institution. The women will probably be more comfortable if you have silent sessions at which they review a list of potential prospects and rate the ones they know by gift range and possible philanthropic interest. At every encounter, the women must be continually assured that they are indispensable and possess the abilities to do a good job, not only for screening prospects but for raising money as well.

Meetings

Meeting structure may be different in a campaign led by women or intended to appeal to women. A number of good books and articles have been written about the different ways in which women lead and manage, including Sally Helgesen's *The Female Advantage: Women's Ways of Leadership* (1990). These styles are important to consider when organizing the cabinet and planning meetings. Many women are more comfortable in nonhierarchical settings and become impatient with cumbersome protocols. Although there are certainly many exceptions, and women may become more competitive as they assume equal status in the corporate world, experience with corporate women so far shows that even those who rise to high positions prefer sharing their power and have a collaborative, collegial style of leadership. Today's corporate women describe their management styles as more participatory, inclusive, and consensus-building than the conventional styles used by males (Bonavoglia, 1991 pp. 14–15). Women's management method is to inspire and influence, not control. Judy B. Rosener of the Graduate School of Management at the University of California, Irvine, describes this as an "interactive" or "transformational" leadership style, as opposed to a traditional male "command and control" style (Rosener, 1990).

Women often want open strategy sessions, and they are willing to admit that they are wrong or do not know the answers. All of this suggests that we should try to make everyone as comfortable as possible by refraining from too much structure and by encouraging "breakout" sessions—relatively unstructured times to relax and share ideas.

Report Meetings

Of all the pieces of a capital campaign, the report meetings and the solicitations are the ones that have changed the most over the years. Report meetings have evolved from competitive sessions where everyone was put on the line to produce names, dates, and figures to meetings where people discuss their successes, their best approaches, and how they might have dealt better with a situation. Some meetings become focus groups and deal with people's perceptions about the institution itself, philanthropy in general, the solicitation process, and parity in giving and decision making. Finding the structure that works best for your constituency and community is most important. Remember to be flexible. Every meeting does not have to be the same, and report meetings that incorporate focus groups are fun. They should be opportunities for people to share and join with others to make things happen.

Report meetings should be held fairly frequently at the beginning so that members do not feel overwhelmed by the magnitude of the task. Above all, report meetings should be purposeful and comfortable. Every meeting should feature a success story to help people feel confident and relaxed about participating.

Solicitations

With women filling at least half of the positions on your campaign committees, you will find that many members have never asked for money in the past. Some fairly extensive training may have to take place. It has been our experience that although they may not admit it, a great many men do not know how to raise money either. This is a good opportunity for people of both genders to be educated. It is important to promote a sense of security among volunteers so that they will be encouraged to take risks. Allow them to make mistakes and share their failures as well as their successes. (Volunteer training is discussed in more detail in Chapter Nine.)

Some points to keep in mind about solicitations are these:

- The fear of rejection is what most bothers women when thinking about asking for a gift. It is important to arrange training sessions that include role playing (ways to do this are described in Chapter Nine). Another possibility is to present a brief script at a session, with the dialogue frozen for discussion at critical points. It is important to choose your language well and not use expressions like "high roller" or "moneybags," which are demeaning and make women uncomfortable.

- Encourage everyone to read about the different ways in which women and men communicate. Handouts and overheads can be prepared about this topic, and training can be conducted by a communication specialist.

- Plan well for the call before it is made, and learn all you can about the prospect. Be sensitive to the details of her relationship with your institution. If she does not appear to be connected enough to be asked for a gift, offer her opportunities to learn more about the organization.

- View prospects as individuals first, then as potential contributors and advocates for your institution.

- Urge development staff and volunteers alike to discover and develop their own personal fundraising and communication style.

- Be sure that each novice is accompanied by someone who has made calls before, either another volunteer or a staff person.

- If the volunteer is new to raising money, a letter can be sent ahead of time requesting a specific amount. That way, at the time of the call, the ask has already been made, and the meeting can be spent talking about the institution. This, of course, assumes that the proper amount of cultivation has taken place prior to sending the letter.

- Have couples call on other couples.
- If a call is made to a married individual, ask if his or her spouse will also make a pledge or if this is a joint gift. Be sure that the spouse is included in the discussion or at least made aware of what is going on and asked to be involved.
- Avoid the appearance of arrogance when talking about the husband's institution to the couple.
- Campaigns are about people, so talk about people's lives, or better yet, bring your prospects to the institution or take program recipients along on your calls.
- Provide plenty of details, and include a carefully presented plan. Be prepared to suggest special projects of interest. Expect probing questions.
- Allow sufficient time for thoughtful reflection before expecting a decision.
- Be prepared to find, as Wellesley did, that women are much less likely to make an annual pledge than men. You may need to ask for the entire amount of the gift to receive it. However, a yearly request will further connect women with the organization and build the relationship.
- Think creatively when you ask for the gift, and describe how it might bring about change or serve entrepreneurial purposes.
- Use an approach based on relationships and responsibilities. Talk about sharing and joining rather than the traditional competitive "do it for the team" appeal.
- Listen to what your prospects are saying. Take their concerns and questions seriously, and make it clear that you value what you have learned from them.
- Believe in your cause to the extent that you can ask others to invest in it. Then you can share your donors' sense of satisfaction as they match their interests with their dollars.

- Be ready to savor the mastery and success of your new volunteers as they become proficient fundraisers.

Campaign Events

You will want to plan campaign events every chance you have and make them causes for celebration. Whether it is a kickoff event, a donor rating session, or a report meeting, make it fun so that your volunteers will want to keep coming to meetings and help raise money for you again. Ask your volunteers what events they would prefer, and be prepared to modify your plans by city or region to reflect your volunteers' interests and the most effective approach.

Recognition and Appreciation

Write personal notes of appreciation throughout the campaign, and ask your campaign leaders to do the same. These handwritten notes should be designed to recognize an individual's work for the cause and the program, as well as their financial support. Taking the time to do this will ultimately enhance the effectiveness of your volunteers and determine how hard they will work for your institution.

Use the names of both husband and wife on all correspondence that might relate to the two of them, and put their individual names on donor plaques and gift listings (unless they request otherwise).

Ask donors how they want to be acknowledged, keeping in mind that women are not as likely as men to want things named after them. Encourage women to step up and allow their names to be used as an inspiration for other donors.

Final Push

All participants like to believe that they have helped put a campaign over the top, and women seem to respond particularly well to this. By asking them again to give and play a part in the campaign's final appeal, you are inviting them to share and join in making something happen.

Adaptability

You will find that your new campaign will never be boring—you will not be doing any one thing in the same way long enough for boredom to set in. The campaign, if it is truly reflective of your institution, will be constantly evolving, and you will need a structure flexible enough to take advantage of new ideas or address problems as they arise. Target and tailor your campaign to your individual prospects and their region. This may mean developing a variety of approaches, but people will be aware that you have made the effort to learn about them and their community. You need not throw out everything that you have done in previous capital campaigns; you need merely modify your techniques. The rewards will not only be increased dollars but also a strengthened institution, thanks to the addition of the formerly neglected values and perspectives of half the population.

Chapter Eleven

Raising Funds from Women: Case Studies

In this chapter we will describe four projects with which we have been closely involved: the Council on Women's Giving of the Bascom Hill Society, University of Wisconsin Foundation; Very Special Arts Wisconsin; A Fund for Women, under the Madison Community Foundation; and Sigma Kappa national sorority. They are four very different experiences, ranging from a commitment of a few months to several years. Through our ongoing research, we have been able to apply several approaches and found that some succeeded and others did not. As a result of these projects, we have refined our plans and strategies for increasing women's gifts. We hope that these vignettes will help you as you begin your plans by alerting you to certain conditions you will face: frustration, creation, education, empowerment, and, most important, the joy of seeing women become literate and enthusiastic about fundraising and giving.

Council on Women's Giving of the Bascom Hill Society, University of Wisconsin Foundation

Martha A. Taylor

The idea began when I shared my frustrations with Jean Manchester-Biddick, the only woman on the foundation's executive committee. I was concerned because the foundation was neither attracting women donors to the board nor reaching out to the graduates of the schools of education, nursing, and family resources—primarily

women. As a result of these early discussions, Jean became the catalyst for the entire effort. She made the lead gift "to support the
activities of women and giving at the University of Wisconsin
Foundation," and this gave credibility to a controversial idea.

Although Jean's idea was radical enough to be considered ahead
of its time, Jean herself enjoyed great respect in the community as
the chief executive officer of a large wholesale meat business in
Madison. Her story is detailed in Chapter Nine. She credits her
UW education with providing her with the skills necessary to reor-
ganize the company, support her family, and enrich herself as a community leader and philanthropist.

We were sure that we would not have any problem marketing
our idea. We knew that women cared deeply about social problems
connected with the education of women and children and with
families in our country. Jean and I agreed that to enact real change
in society, major institutions of higher education not only must be
involved but in fact must lead the way. The University of Wisconsin, with its programs of significant national impact, could be a con-
sequential vehicle in reaching this goal. Its women graduates had
the financial resources, so why were they not giving? Was it something about the women themselves or about the way the UW Foundation conducted its fundraising?

"The final capstone in our resolve to do something," Jean
recalls, "was the feasibility study for our capital campaign. The
School of Family Resources and Consumer Sciences—my school—
was rated low on a list of donor priorities, and a few comments were
made in passing that maybe it should be dropped from the campaign. It was not surprising that the school was rated low, despite
its excellent academics: only six out of the one hundred people
interviewed for the campaign feasibility study were women. After
the meeting, we called the dean, who got reassurances that the
school would not be dropped."

Jean and I tried to identify women to participate in another
study, but we just did not have women "in the loop," with the influ-

ence and resources to give major gifts. Although subsequent studies have shown that women gave 36 percent of the total gifts to the
university, we were caught short. Jean had served on the foundation's membership committee for years, and we both had forwarded
names of women for the board. But when looking up women's gift
records, we saw very little activity. Men were often put on the board
simply because of their potential. Why not women, too? we won-
dered. Our efforts to recruit more women were foundering.

At the same time, we learned of some colleges who were actually discussing whether women students should be admitted at the
same rate as men—all because of the perception that women do
not or will not give as much as men. How much was myth, we won-
dered, and how much reality?

Involving Key Leaders

We were determined to do something, and the first step was
to involve our key leaders. I met with each woman individually.
Following that, I met with a group of six women donors who
had each given at least $10,000 to the university, as well as Mary
Ann Shaw, vice president for development of the United Way
of Dane County and wife of the president of the UW system,
Kenneth Shaw. Jean chaired the meeting and successfully articu-
lated our goal of overcoming, from within the foundation and the
university, the political process that resulted in women's being overlooked and underrepresented among major donors.

Several organizational options were discussed, and program
models were sought. However, none was found that could be
applied at a major coeducational institution. It became clear that
we would have to invent our own program.

Our initial gathering of six expanded to twenty-five individuals through personal contacts and discussion. Face to face, I had
asked each of them to join the council and sought their gift support
if they were not already members of the Bascom Hill Society.

Although these contacts were made outside my regular schedule, I was delighted to find these women genuinely pleased to see me. Many had not had prior contact with the foundation. Jean's example in her philanthropy, her quiet leadership style, and her leadership gift supplied the urgent and substantive credibility that motivated the others to join her.

I also met with every female member of the foundation board to seek endorsement. These women also made large gift commitments during the campaign. Other key supporters on campus included Katherine Lyall, who succeeded Kenneth Shaw as UW system president; Judith Ward, vice president of the UW system; and her husband, David Ward, chancellor of the University of Wisconsin, Madison. These people helped create an atmosphere of acceptance that made women want to be involved. The backing of David Ward and other key male volunteers was an important part of our acceptance on campus.

Defining the Council and Dealing with the Issues

The council was launched in 1988 with the following fundamental goals:

- To raise significant sums from women and men to benefit the University of Wisconsin, Madison, and to encourage women to give major gifts in their own names and for purposes of their own choosing
- To encourage and facilitate the advancement of women in volunteer leadership positions for the Bascom Hill Society and the UW Foundation
- To advance the role of women as philanthropists in society in general

As the women dealt with the question of how to work within

the foundation while at the same time setting up a separate organization just for women, discussions became lengthy and sometimes heated. To mollify everyone, it was decided that rather than raise money strictly for "women's issues" or a specific women's project list, the council would raise money to benefit any university project designated by the donor.

After some debate, the council decided to incorporate within the university's major gift club, the Bascom Hill Society, with a $10,000 minimum gift required for membership, to emphasize that this group was not an auxiliary of any kind.

A third issue that arose was whether the women would raise money only from other women or from men also. The council chose not to exclude men from their fundraising efforts. However, it soon discovered that women made good prospects because they had usually not been asked for major gifts and hence were not already in someone else's prospect file.

We also determined early on that the council was not to be a recognition group—not all women giving at the $10,000 or greater level would automatically become members. The council is an active committee of women donors who encourage others to follow their example. For some, this means active solicitation. For others, it means giving their gift and lending their good name to the concept. Certainly, the combination of generous giver and active volunteer is the most powerful.

Exploring the Topic and Building Relationships

Mary Ann Shaw generously hosted three luncheons at her home, the UW president's residence, for council members and prospects. The first two events featured a prominent engineering faculty member speaking about her microchip research and work to recruit more women into the sciences. After the presentation, a council member served as facilitator at each table for a discussion on the following questions:

- How would you like the University of Wisconsin, Madison, to help address the problems of our society?
- How are decisions about charitable giving made in your household?
- If you were giving $100,000 to the university, what types of projects would you fund? (The amount was later upped to $1 million.)

The questions were designed to connect the women to the university by asking for their assistance in ways that the university could address. We were interested in getting women to think about the problems of society, how they currently contributed their money, and the consequences and emotions involved in giving a large gift. After lunch, the facilitators reported on the lively discussions at their tables.

One of our luncheons was attended by a photographer from the *New York Times Magazine*. The article, "Alma Maters Court Their Daughters," by Ann Matthews, a UW Madison alumna, ran in the April 7, 1991, issue and focused national attention on the program and the women's philanthropy movement.

Soon there were too many prospects for one staff member alone to solicit. At this point, the council resolved to train its members as volunteer fundraisers. The training program, as described in Chapter Nine, was launched in the winter of 1992.

National Forums

The council's active leadership group, led by Jean Manchester-Biddick, determined that a special forum for UW alumnae from all over the country needed to be held to provide a distinct focus on women and philanthropy. Joan Fisher, director of development for B'nai B'rith Women, in Washington, D.C., gave an impassioned speech at our first forum about the needs of society from a current and historical perspective and why women must be philanthropists.

Council-Supported Projects

The council has been helpful in supporting several University of Wisconsin women's initiatives, including a women's alumnae group called Cabinet 99 and the Center for Women and Philanthropy in the School of Family Resources and Consumer Sciences. Individual council members provided seed money for these projects. Members of the council also serve on the steering committee for the center and formed the planning committee for a national conference to establish an agenda for women and philanthropy. This conference, sponsored by the center, was held at the Johnson Foundation's Wingspread Conference Center in Racine, Wisconsin, in October 1992.

A National and Local City Model

UW's $400 million capital campaign coincided perfectly with the next stage of council activities. We wanted to keep the original council and add other groups nationally to form what would be known as the national steering committee, which would meet annually.

We also decided to establish local city chapters, the prototype to be the group based in Madison. All women actively serving on the council were invited to serve as well on the Madison campaign committee, which eventually raised $60 million in the five-year campaign ending in December 1992. The council members who served on the committee took great pride in their efforts to reach that goal and realized that fundraising for major gifts is a long-term process and that their role is one of ongoing volunteer work for the foundation.

With the campaign at end, we are fine-tuning the structure of the council and exploring how to launch our efforts in other cities. The council work will continue to be integrated into the entire foundation and university effort.

Financial Education

The council recognized early on that one of its primary missions is to educate women about finances in order to direct their volunteerism toward making major monetary gifts. These educational sessions have since become a major focus of the council. One of the highlights of a session was a presentation by Tracy Gary, director of Resourceful Women, an organization that helps women of wealth manage their money and their philanthropy. This session, which took place in July 1993, is described in Chapter Twelve. That fall, the council presented three programs dealing with university gift opportunities and motivations, how to give a major gift, and financial and investment training.

Significant Gifts

The six volunteer founders of the council each made a significant gift commitment, and these gifts and others from women were announced at each meeting. The dollar amount and the donor's name were not mentioned without prior consent.

The first key gifts were from Jean Manchester-Biddick and Kay Vaughan. Manchester-Biddick's gifts were $100,000 for the Center for Family Excellence and $5,000 for work on women and giving. These had the leverage of $1 million because they were gifts that showed faith in the concept. Vaughan had previously given, with her husband, two professorships at the university in departments in which their fathers had been professors. Vaughan's 1991 gift of $25,000 established the Center for Women and Philanthropy and funded the Wingspread Conference.

The cochairs of the Madison committee also conferred important early gifts: Katherine S. Nordeen, retired assistant athletic director, gave for a fund in her name for women's athletics, and Marjorie Tobias, for the Center for Jewish Studies, in both her name and that of her husband.

Mary Ann Bast, a successful young stockbroker, set a new format for giving. We wanted to have permanently endowed scholarships in women's names while offering donors the opportunity to meet and encourage the recipients. Bast committed a $50,000 endowment over future years. While her daughter is in college, she is giving $2,000 annually, with half going to the endowment and half to a student. Bast is grateful for the joy of meeting the recipients. Her involvement with the students of the business school has led her to join other businesswomen in a new mentoring program for female business students.

Phyllis Lovrien, vice president of the Oscar Mayer Corporation, although not a graduate of the University of Wisconsin, has become involved with the council and the Madison campaign by making a significant commitment to fund an annual lectureship at the school of business for outstanding women business leaders. She told me, "I want to thank you for opening up this opportunity to me. You gave me permission to follow my dreams and hopes of helping younger women." She also greatly influenced the dean of the business school to establish an executive master's of business administration (M.B.A.) program.

Marla Ahlgrimm, a young entrepreneur and owner of a national pharmaceutical company, was an early leader who gave a scholarship in her own name to the school of pharmacy. She is not only a council pillar but also the youngest person to serve on the Bascom Hill Society's executive committee and the only woman entrepreneur on the pharmacy school's board of visitors. Ahlgrimm has also gone to extraordinary measures to help launch Cabinet 99 and a club to promote women's athletics.

The council's efforts have also brought new supporters to the university community. For example, a retired woman called on by a council member stated that she was not considering making a major donation. However, the member graciously brought her to events, and a year later the woman gave a cash gift of $25,000 and deferred gifts of more than $100,000. Other significant gifts from women influenced by the council's efforts include donations to the arts, the arboretum, and the law, education, and library schools, among others.

Results

In six years, the council has seen the emergence of women donors and volunteer fundraisers as an important source of new money for the university. By continuously highlighting women's efforts in publications and at events, the council has convinced the university that this movement deserves its full support and approval. Unquestionably, the council has emerged as a national model for involving women that can be applied at many other educational and nonprofit institutions.

Reviewing the formation of the council, we note the following ideas that worked well:

- A lead gift was secured from a well-respected woman member of the foundation who was passionately involved in getting the council under way.
- Having key members and backers, including men, on campus increased acceptance and helped avoid the "women's auxiliary" image.
- Internal support was provided by colleagues who took on extra work for the council because they knew few resources had been allocated.
- National attention from the *New York Times Magazine* gave the program authenticity and built tremendous momentum.

Similar opportunities can exist for other groups using state and local media.

- The questions asked at the luncheons opened women's eyes to the possibilities of their own personal philanthropy and helped motivate them to make gifts in areas of their interest.

- The two biennial forums have been great successes. Men were invited to the second one, including the chief executive officer of the UW Foundation and the president of the Madison Community Foundation.

- By not limiting its efforts to the funding of women's programs, the council reassured others that it was working for the benefit of the entire institution.

- Synchronization with the capital campaign enabled the council members to become involved in a major fundraising effort.

- As a result of the successes of the Women's Council, more foundation leadership positions have been filled by women: in 1992, one-half of nominees to the foundation were women, compared to none in 1991 and one or two annually prior to that. Thus the council has been an important factor in transforming development procedures at this major educational institution.

Very Special Arts Wisconsin

Sondra C. Shaw and Martha A. Taylor

Very Special Arts Wisconsin (VSA WIS), which provides programs in the arts for people with disabilities, has an annual budget of nearly $1 million, including in-kind services, raised through board involvement and the efforts of its extremely competent president, Kay Lindblade. Chairing the executive committee of this decade-old organization is Sue Ann Thompson, sixth-grade teacher and first lady of the state of Wisconsin. Sue Ann, who has great sensitivity and commitment to people, was attracted to the organization in 1987 by its educational mission. Our story here begins with the VSA WIS board's concern that the foundation lacked a reserve. Sue Ann volunteered to spearhead a rainy-day fund of $100,000.

When we were asked to volunteer in this effort, we saw several reasons why it would be a good project for fundraising by women. First, both of the leaders were strong women with good name recognition and contacts; second, the program touched women's interests because it involved helping people, mainly children; third, it was an opportunity for women to create something, in this case a special fund for the organization.

A model of an all-woman fundraising team already existed with Maddie Levitt's successful program at Drake University to raise money to restore the Old Main auditorium.

Kay and Sue Ann recruited seven prominent women from around the state, and we met at the executive residence in the spring of 1993. We soon learned that we would have to scrap our initial plan of having the women form their own campaign. Group members had such varied experiences with fundraising and giving that they themselves still needed to have their sights raised. Though we could not depend on them to come up with the money strategy, we felt that they still needed to create the design.

Challenges and Problems

We found that our major challenge was to keep the group focused on the target of $100,000, fighting the tendency to take the bake sale approach to fundraising. The president already had her hands full and did not need the extra burden of coordinating twenty to thirty people to raise a relatively small amount of money. Although she clearly possessed the kinds of skills that would have allowed her to raise the money herself, she more than any of us knew that by successfully completing this effort, she would be extending the foundation's donor base to people who had never even heard of VSA WIS. Her challenge was to convince the women that they could give and ask for major gifts of $5,000 and above.

Our final problem was to raise the sights of some of the women on the committee regarding how much they themselves could give. When we talked about the fact that in most committees, the members themselves are responsible for giving at least 20 percent of the money, it was apparent that some had not considered this and felt that their volunteer time would stand in for actual monetary gifts.

We spent a great deal of very worthwhile time at the first meeting connecting and learning about one another and about VSA WIS. It is never enough just to say, "This is a worthwhile program." If women are asked to raise money, they want to be sure that they know all about the project. The most moving part of the day was a presentation by an adult artist with a disability whose work is part of the VSA WIS collection. Through this gifted man, the members had a real encounter with a person served by the program.

We also had a long and entertaining discussion about what to name the group. Sue Ann came up with the Bridge the Future campaign, and the committee members would be Bridge Tenders. Details like these were very important to the women creating their own campaign—they wanted to be involved and part of everything. They also wanted to have fun in the process.

By the end of the four-hour meeting, it had been determined that committee members would give Kay the names of prospects and others who might serve on the committee. Both men and women would be asked to give. The second meeting was set, again at the executive residence, for the following month. In the meantime, Kay was to solicit personal gifts from the committee members.

In an analysis following the first meeting, we identified the problems as how to raise the women's expectations about their own gift size and about how much they should ask others for, what size the committee should be, and who should lead the group.

Our second meeting designated a chairperson, established a

time line, and determined that the committee would be kept fairly small but flexible enough to add people who expressed an interest.

The third meeting was planned for the day of the Very Special Arts Wisconsin State Festival in Madison. Committee members and prospects were invited to attend the opening ceremonies, visit workshops where children were creating art, and enjoy an outdoor lunch with a thousand children from all over the state. The women especially enjoyed interacting with the children, many of whom came up and hugged them and asked them to autograph their T-shirts, which had been produced especially for that day. Kay recalls, "The state festival was very important because key women were there and could see how VSA WIS really does make a difference." They were off to a fine start.

Kay, who has a knack for understanding what pleases women, came up with unique but inexpensive ways to recognize the volunteers' efforts. At both the first and third meetings, she gave them gifts—note cards done by the VSA WIS artists and T-shirts. These gifts not only pleased committee members but also helped connect them with the project and with one another. This was all part of having fun, and that was just what the committee planned over the summer, with two gatherings to acquaint people with the program and solicit gifts.

At each meeting, some hesitation was expressed about asking for large sums of money, as well as about the amount that committee members would be expected to give. However, major doubts were resolved through others' commitment to the effort and their encouragement to solicit gifts and "think big."

In time, the women became very serious about the effort. At the first summer meeting, soliciting techniques were discussed, along with the event agenda. Everyone contributed thoughtful, practical ideas. It was apparent that the women were spending some time considering the best approach. The most interesting part was the personal style and flexibility of the members. It was quite acceptable for them to use bits and pieces of the suggestions and techniques, depending on what they were most comfortable with and what they felt would work best for them. For example, some of the members thought that they would make the ask at the events so that people could join together in giving; others wanted only to acquaint people with VSA WIS and then call on them personally afterward.

During their discussions, we could sense the role playing going on in their minds as they contemplated their guests, the type of event, and the location. Only a couple of times at this meeting did we need to remind the women to think big.

Organization

The committee set up six recommended gift levels, from $1,000 to $50,000 and above. Interestingly, no one they solicited asked about recognition plaques or donor lists. That kind of recognition was not important to the women donors. When we asked what they themselves would like in recognition of their efforts, the committee members suggested artwork by one of the VSA WIS artists. That was the most meaningful to them.

Also at the first summer meeting, the committee updated the time line, establishing the campaign conclusion for the end of October. Sue Ann suggested that a celebration be held at the executive residence in conjunction with a home football game at which VSA students would be participating with the UW marching band.

A memo was mailed to the committee on August 1, stating that $51,550 had been raised and giving dates for coming events: a luncheon in Milwaukee underwritten by a member's corporation and a reception at a residence in Lake Geneva. Sue Ann and Kay spoke at both events, as well as two VSA WIS participants—one a poet and the other a painter. Apart from this, each meeting followed a different format. The Milwaukee luncheon was straightforward and informative; the Lake Geneva gathering was more subtle and did not include much discussion about follow-up calls. The meetings were geared to the comfort level of the hostess and the style of the guests. Altogether, the two gatherings raised $10,000.

In September the committee received an invitation from Sue Ann to a continental breakfast at the executive residence, followed by a tour of Frank Lloyd Wright's home and school, Taliesin, in Spring Green. Sue Ann also serves on the Taliesin commission, which is raising funds to preserve the home.

At the conclusion of the successful VSA WIS project, which met its goal primarily through gifts from women or contacts made by women, our review showed that the following ideas worked well:

- The women created their own project and thus had a continuing connection and interest in it.

- The women enjoyed one another's company and wanted each event to be a celebration.

- They appreciated the small gifts and considered these, along with the special relationships with one another, quite adequate rewards.

- Several women who had never before considered giving large gifts or asking others for them were thrilled with their success.

- No single "right" way to solicit was set down.

- Although the creation process was arduous at the outset, it gained momentum once everyone was educated and connected.

- Members of the committee of fifteen committed half the total amount raised—much more than the suggested 20 percent that had so startled them originally.

- Fundraising and campaign concepts were introduced at one meeting and built on at the next so that the women could reflect on and get used to the new ideas.

After the final goal-reaching celebration, Sue Ann was already planning for the future and looking to see what the Bridge Tenders could do next. The women had so much fun that they did not want to part company. They were enthusiastically reaching out to take on the next project—a sure sign of success.

A Fund for Women

Sondra C. Shaw and Martha A. Taylor

Jane Coleman, executive director of the Madison Community Foundation, was part of the initial focus groups we convened for an article about career women and their giving. This experience piqued her interest in women's philanthropy, but she says her real inspiration came from participating as a facilitator at the 1992 Wingspread Conference on Women and Philanthropy. Because Jane is a very contemplative but busy person, she knew that there was a right thing for her to do. After some deliberation, she sent out a letter inviting one hundred women to a meeting to discuss the possibility of creating a women's fund within the community foundation. The letter requested a gift of $1,000 from each interested participant. Jane's goal was to have one hundred women each give $1,000 to constitute a nucleus fund of $100,000. Although that may run contrary to most fundraising methods, the Madison community values modesty and democracy above all else, and it was believed preferential to establish broad-based support rather than garner a lot of money from a select few.

The Process

Thirty women came to the first meeting, several having already committed $1,000. A brief meeting agenda was distributed, along with lists of attenders who had committed, those were not yet ready to do so, and those who were not interested.

Jane opened the meeting by explaining her interest in the subject and how she became involved. She asked us to describe briefly what kind of experience or knowledge we had about women and philanthropy, then opened the meeting to questions. This was the period of real exploration and creation for the women, although some felt decidedly uncomfortable with the "fuzziness" of the process. A few of the women would have preferred reacting on a specific topic to the open-ended format. Nevertheless, the discussion at this first meeting tended to focus on possibilities for the name of the fund, its internal organization, and targeting suggestions for future funds.

Jane was determined, however, to make this initiative something special for Madison and not a copy of some other fund's system. A steering committee, developed at the initial meeting, volunteered to begin working on the organization. Jane asked the volunteers to consider the names of other prospects: those women would receive letters of invitation mentioning the name of the person who had suggested them. A few more people pledged or contributed money, and the meeting ended with the promise to call everyone back together to review the steering committee's recommendations.

Over the next couple of months, the steering committee of ten, three of whom were attorneys, met and chose the name A Fund for Women. Committee members felt that they needed more information about the members' interests, however, and also wanted to educate themselves about philanthropy and its possibilities for women. In particular, they wanted to consider how to empower women to take control of their money and direct it toward their interests.

Jane was also a firm believer in women having fun together, and because she had enjoyed our earlier focus groups, she asked us to conduct focus groups for the second meeting with new donors and prospects. The idea was not only to find out more about what the women were interested in but also to help them bond and connect. Indeed, that was precisely what happened.

Jane announced that sixty women had pledged or given a total of $61,000 toward the goal. We explained our current projects and research on women and philanthropy and gave a brief history of women philanthropists. We also distributed a questionnaire about the women's interest and support levels, asking them to fill out and return the forms by the end of the meeting. During this time, we could sense the women's interest and their eagerness to get into the focus groups to talk more.

We conducted the focus groups with the help of two other members of the fund, using the same questions as presented in Chapter Seven. University students were asked to take notes and record the sessions. Everyone had a most enjoyable time, and many people stayed beyond the two hours allotted to the meeting.

The general philanthropy questions elicited the following summarized responses:

- Philanthropy equals altruism, sharing, belonging, obligation, and making a difference. Philanthropy is not intrinsic to power.

- The women's primary philanthropic goal was the local distribution of their money to women and children.

- The women wanted to give back, influence, share, and improve the quality of life. They saw educational support as a way to do that.

- The women felt that young people should learn early about philanthropy but knew that some successful people learn later in life as they develop the desire to give back what they have reaped. They felt that adults have an obligation to teach their children about giving through special occasions like Thanksgiving or by making gift giving a family matter.

- Women give differently at different ages, depending on their stage in life as well as their marital and family status. At every stage, though, women understand the need for change and will respond to relevant issues.

- Women have not traditionally been perceived as givers and

hence have few philanthropic role models. Many older women, in particular, do not understand their giving potential, and a great deal of education is needed.

- Although women own 60 percent of the nation's wealth, they do not necessarily control it. Men are perceived as controlling women's money. Power and control issues need to be addressed.

We asked specific questions about A Fund for Women's organization and its role in the community. Most of the women responded that they became interested in the fund simply because Jane had asked them. She is respected as one of the city's philanthropic leaders and a role model. They felt that because Jane had asked them, it was worthwhile learning about what she had in mind. Many women also liked the unaffected idea of getting together with women of all ages who care about the same issues. Some were curious about how women would work together, knowing that women generally view organization and management differently from men.

The women said that they felt empowered to be with other women working with a great potential for change, though they were still somewhat uncomfortable with the lack of organization and detail at that point. Most of the women wanted some continuing connection with the organization but were not sure what that might be.

A spirited discussion took place about power as related to both money and women. Negative and positive responses were written on a flip chart, and Jane commented, "We all bring enormous baggage to these words as they deal with philanthropy. It won't ever be just the dollars women give that are convincing: it will be women's power to give."

At the next steering committee meeting, Tracy Gary, of Resourceful Women, spoke about the necessity of being well organized. That would involve taking the time to establish a mission statement, conduct strategic planning, develop fundraising goals, and address the need for diversity within the organization. She recommended building the board two members at a time and identifying early on leaders who would "hang in there for three years" as organizers and donors. She also strongly urged the fund to contact the National Network of Women's Funds (NNWF) in Minneapolis for technical assistance.

Tracy also cautioned that existing women's groups might feel that their donor base is threatened by the founding of a new group. She offered the following suggestions: tell prospective donors that you want them to keep supporting their other organizations at current levels but to give the largest gift they have ever given to A Fund for Women, promise the other organizations that their lists will not be used, and keep in touch with the other organizations through personal contacts with their leaders to show appreciation of all that they have done and are doing.

Following this meeting, the steering committee decided to join the NNWF and to contact other women's funds for materials and input. They also decided to hold a fall meeting for all Fund for Women contributors and prospects featuring Carol Mollner, executive director of the NNWF, as the keynote speaker. Committees were established, including "financial literacy" and philanthropic education, grant making, diversity, and development.

We had accomplished much but still had not reached our goal—we had collected $84,000 from seventy-eight people. The committee also realized that even if we reached $100,000, at current interest rates only about $5,000 could be distributed annually, which could not have much impact. In addition, Jane was uncomfortable about raising money for the fund when she was director of the entire community foundation, but in truth she alone had the contacts and drive necessary to get us to our goal.

What we needed was a woman or two who were willing to make a three-year commitment of $10,000 each, which the fund could use for grants as it was growing its endowment. Following the meeting, one of the women present actually made such a commitment. Jane contacted three or four other prospects, including one widower who made the grant in his wife's name. By the September meeting, not only was the fund nearing its goal of $100,000, but $30,000 had been pledged as an annual fund grant for the next three years, and an additional $5,000 seemed likely.

Moving Ahead

Now we were off and running. The group had accomplished a great deal in seven months. It had not been easy, and the steering committee did not really begin perking until its last two meetings. Plenty remained to be done: we needed further work on organizational structure, increased fundraising to get the endowment up to $600,000 by the end of three years, and strategic planning. The issues of whether the fund should continue as part of the community foundation or become a separate entity and whether it should invest in socially responsible corporations must be dealt with. As of summer 1994 it seemed likely that the fund would follow the lead of women's funds in Philadelphia, Milwaukee, and other cities in sponsoring an annual event to obtain the rest of the money to reach its fundraising goal.

The matter of conscientious investment was considered at each of the meetings, and Jane strongly believes that women tend to be more concerned about this issue than men do. She cited two women donors to the fund who, she believed, would not give additional amounts if the monies were not invested with a social conscience. Agreements had been reached on such an impressive number of things, including the mission statement, the education plan, the committee structure, and the steering committee membership, that there is no doubt that we will find a solution to the investment issue as well.

In summary, we believe that the following ideas worked well:

- A woman who is well respected in the community asked others to join, and they did so out of regard for her, even though intentions were unclear.

- A list was presented at the first meeting showing who had already committed, so the women felt that they were joining with others.

- It was possible to pledge over a period of time, so more individuals could be involved.

- The women were allowed to create their own entity, which drew them in and made them feel part of the whole.

- A substantial amount of money was set aside specifically for grants to help the fund gain visibility while still getting under way and building its base.

- Women attorneys were very much a part of the effort, just as they were in the 1992 political campaigns, and can often be counted on to support grassroots issues, especially those affecting women.

Sigma Kappa National Sorority

Sondra C. Shaw

Sigma Kappa had been conducting an annual campaign, called the Loyalty Fund, since 1981. Nonetheless, its foundation, created in 1962 as the philanthropic and educational arm of the sorority, had remained fairly inactive until its incorporation and the arrival in 1990 of Paula Jenkins-Williams as director of development. Two years later, Jean Elder was elected president.

Paula had been working for the sorority as public relations director prior to her promotion and had virtually no development experience. However, she was a natural in her new position and a very quick study. She felt a personal obligation to establish an endowment for the people who will come after her, and she knew that the only way to do that was to begin a planned-giving program. Within three years, she increased the Loyalty Fund's net by $59,000 and developed an uncomplicated planned-giving program, as well as new literature. She observes, "Our donor base had great potential. Unfortunately, donors making gifts of $500 had been acknowledged and treated like donors making $25 gifts. Our first challenge was to segment the donor base on cumulative giving levels and start the top donors on a different track of cultivation and solicitation. In its first year, the top donor segment consisted of 552 prospects. Three years later, that segment had nearly doubled to 1,054 prospects."

Jean Elder, a former member of the Michigan State University education faculty, was a widely known and respected education consultant. Her presence, political insight, and organization skills complemented and enhanced Paula's hardworking enthusiasm, professionalism, and instinct. Both wanted to develop a broad-based program beginning with sorority women still in college to get them used to giving, to cement their connection to the sorority, and ultimately to develop them into annual givers. The program would focus on major gift prospects in the expectation of mounting a capital campaign in three to five years. "I believe," Jean explains, "that as women's sororities look to the year 2000 and beyond, we have to accept that we can't continue raising fees. We must do broad-based fundraising, or our programs won't flourish."

Many sororities have national development programs, though this is a fairly recent phenomenon. All sororities, however, have projects beyond scholarships that hold great appeal to women as donors. Quite a few sponsor programs in such areas as breast cancer, arthritis, and juvenile diabetes research and the Children's Miracle Network Telethon. One of Sigma Kappa's projects, for example, funds research for Alzheimer's disease. The sorority annually awards $50,000 to $60,000, primarily in small grants and principally to women.

All of the elements were in place for a successful women's

fundraising program: eighty thousand educated and fairly affluent members with fond memories of their college years; established projects ranging from scholarships to the environment, gerontology, and Alzheimer's research; plus a strong staff and president. The missing elements were a foundation board and a national council that understood fundraising and gave significantly to the sorority; a plan or goal beyond the Loyalty Fund, which really raised money merely to run the foundation; and recognition and understanding of the foundation on the part of collegians or graduates. All in all, fundraising had not been taken seriously by the sorority's governing groups, who regarded it more as a volunteer activity than one with the potential to raise large sums of money.

The First Indianapolis Meeting

To counter this attitude, Jean appointed a seven-member national development committee, which met for two days in spring 1993 to formulate a comprehensive plan. Their goals were to maintain fundraising momentum by creating more scholarships, to get women into the habit of giving, to increase annual giving, to promote the projects funded by the national sorority, to expand the planned-giving program, and to prepare for a major gift campaign.

This committee made decisions fairly swiftly. No doubt this was due to several factors: Jean's competence and composure, Paula's organization of materials, the fact that the committee members had traveled from various geographical areas and had a very short time in which to get things accomplished, and, as one of the volunteer members, my professional fundraising experience, which the others respected.

Over the two days, we worked very hard and agreed on most issues. The few points of contention involved matters of recognition: lifetime versus annual listings of gifts and the use of tangible means of appreciation. However, the discussions continued as planning proceeded and specifics were established. To encourage larger gifts, a new plan for annual giving was created: beyond the former top level of $5,000 were added two new levels, $10,000 and $25,000.

Giving Clubs

To stimulate graduating seniors to give—something that universities do very well—the committee instituted a program called the Five Star Pledge, using the sorority star as the program symbol. Following the program, senior sorority sisters would be asked to pledge $225 over a five-year period.

Perhaps the single most successful outcome of the conference was the establishment of a three-year pledge program. The committee wanted to encourage women to give more than they had before and to consider a multiyear commitment that could be increased at the end. The committee also wanted to prepare members for solicitation of a major gift following fulfillment of the pledge.

We decided to call this next stage the Pearl Club, after the sorority's most prominent gemstone. Members of the club could pledge one, two, or three pearls, each representing $1,000, over three years. It was agreed that personal solicitation was crucial to the program's success.

The Pearl Club was initiated with astonishing results at a board and council meeting attended by fourteen members the following fall. The presenter explained the club and noted that all present should join to demonstrate 100 percent participation by the board and council by the time the program was announced nationally. Two foundation members quietly made their pledges on the spot and then solicited the rest of the members personally during the lunch break. Instead of being asked to pledge money, the women were asked to join the Pearl Club and allowed to select the number of pearls they wanted to pledge. This method proved strikingly successful and made the women feel that they were pledging much as they had when they joined their sorority. Not one person declined, and when the results were presented, the council members individually stood and made their pledges without being asked. All in all, the pledges exceeded the women's previous contributions by $15,000.

Other elements of the program were a more comprehensive planned-giving program, called the Horizon Society, and a major-gift program to help fund all major projects, especially scholarships. Scholarships are essential to sororities because they encourage young women to join, and Sigma Kappa needed to increase their number from fifteen to at least twenty-five, a goal established at the national convention the following year.

Recognition remains a problem. Some of the women were in favor of continuing the practice of giving women ribbons, color-coded according to gift size, at conventions for lifetime contributions to the foundation as low as $25 and ribbons representing only $250 in lifetime giving gained entrance to a special reception. Others felt that recognizing such small contributions keeps women from thinking in terms of larger gifts. As chair of the development committee, I hope to convert this program into one to support a scholarship at conventions, with higher levels required to receive a ribbon.

By and large, however, the committee was quite willing to think big and stretch the concepts of giving. Members became much more knowledgeable about all aspects of development during the two days, including recognizing the need for personal solicitation. Because the staff is so small, one person suggested that each committee, foundation, and council member submit her travel schedule over the next few months so that she could be matched up with donors and prospects living in the parts of the country being visited.

In reviewing the progress made and the ideas that worked well for this organization, we note the following:

- Using the pearl as a symbol for the three-year pledge club reminded the women of their sorority pins and deflected attention from money during the solicitation.

- Personal solicitation worked particularly well in this membership organization.

- Some of the more unsophisticated discussions that had taken place in the other groups were avoided because of the direct participation of a volunteer who was a professional fundraiser as well as a donor.

- A strong team spirit developed, as the women had little time in which to work hard, think big, and be collaborative and helpful.

Conclusion

Although these four case studies differed greatly, certain similarities were apparent: the most successful groups offered the women a chance to get to know one another personally and to have fun. Yet these were not frivolous activities, and all four groups were dedicated to making a difference.

The women may have been timorous at first about fundraising and their abilities to do it, but they all quickly accepted and even embraced the concept. They were not afraid to ask questions or invite help. Furthermore, as they gained in confidence and grew in success, their sense of individual and group pride increased. Each member felt important to the organization.

Although each group had a chair, none of the organizations or meetings was conducted in a hierarchical manner. The women were willing to share power and ask for guidance from one another. Meanwhile, the leaders assumed their roles in highly independent ways without sacrificing their feminine qualities.

Along with the other members of these committees, we also learned some concepts through trial and error:

- Establishing a clear committee structure, mission statement, volunteer job descriptions, and terms of office will keep volunteers interested and involved.

- A one-on-one approach is better for women who are not comfortable discussing philanthropic decisions openly.

- At a coeducational institution, women on the development staff should not be assigned to the women's group full time but should have the work as part of regular activities.

- Women with limited fundraising experience should not be encouraged to structure their own campaign from the start.

- It is wise to consult with similar groups early on to learn from their experiences.

- Because many women are relatively uninformed about financial matters, a strong and knowledgeable person—possibly a woman accountant—should be appointed to the board or council.

It is important that programs aimed at women as donors become part of all institutions, including cultural and service organizations, without being considered "little projects to keep women happy." The bigger picture shows that women want to feel involved before they give and that they need to be educated about turning their volunteerism into giving and asking for money. By pulling women aside and setting up special classes or groups, we can train them to take their place in the mainstream. This is leadership training as well as philanthropic education, which benefits both the institution and the women donors themselves. Women should be recognized and hailed by institutions and organizations for their contributions of money, expertise, and vision.

Chapter Twelve

Working with Women of Wealth

Tracy Gary's concern about the unequal distribution of wealth in our society started when she was nine years old. She recalls asking her nanny one day how much money she made and being shocked to learn that the nanny's salary was $75 for a sixty-hour week. Tracy's own father made one hundred times that amount participating in one board meeting a month, playing golf, and attending social functions. Tracy points to that revelation as her first lesson in social injustice, a prime motivator in her philanthropy ever since.

A dozen years later, she received her own share of the family's wealth from her mother, a Pillsbury, and her father, a major stockholder in General Telephone and Electric. A $2 million inheritance can be accompanied by a host of questions and decisions that for anyone can be overwhelming; for a twenty-one-year-old woman in the 1970s, it was uncharted territory. What was she to do with so much money?

Some of Tracy's initial challenges were the typical barriers to women's giving, as described in Chapter Five. Her mother had "gone off to learn about money" during World War II, according to Tracy, and became a stockbroker because she was concerned that Wall Street would collapse without men to run it. Nonetheless, Tracy herself had grown up relatively uninformed about financial matters. She also experienced the uncertainty and uneasiness that many wealthy people share when confronting the subjects of money and power.

After struggling to come to terms with her own privileged position, she has spent the past two decades helping other women of wealth understand their finances and their philanthropy. Personally committed to social action, Tracy believes that women should designate their gifts where their interests lie, whether it be the environment, culture, education, or social action. One way in which she helps women live up to their philanthropic potential is through an organization she founded, Resourceful Women.

Tracy focuses her philanthropy and her work on programs that serve women and girls. She is also motivated by a powerful entrepreneurial interest that reveals itself in the fifteen nonprofits that she has helped found, including the National Network of Women's Funds. As she travels the country, educating women about money and its potential as a force for change, Tracy hopes that her entrepreneurial spirit will inspire other women to give as well.

Many of the ideas that Tracy uses when conducting seminars for women of wealth are valuable for us to consider when establishing programs in our own institutions. She offers insight into the women's perspectives regarding their finances and their charity, as well as practical tips for learning more about and educating our own women prospects and donors.

Giving Away Three-Quarters of Principal

Although Tracy Gary may not have picked up her mother's financial management skills early on, she learned a lesson from her mother that has been even more important. She learned the value of working for and giving back to the less fortunate. Even today, her mother raises $1 million annually for New York City's Boys' Club and nearly as much for a suburban hospital. Tracy also identifies her godchildren as inspirations "because they are about the future, and I do this work for the future."

Tracy's keen intellect and curiosity, combined with an education at Sarah Lawrence in the late 1960s, helped provide her with leadership qualities and an open mind about gender and racial issues. However, she realized that "if it was difficult for me to deal with inherited wealth, what must it be like for women who haven't had the nurturing and training I received?" She watched other women turn over their decision making to male financial planners and decided that that was not for her. Tracy wanted to take control of her money.

The first thing she did was examine how her money was invested. To her horror, she discovered that much of it was in the stocks of defense contractors who were involved in the Vietnam War. Because she opposed the war, she divested herself of the stocks and chose one of the best investments she has ever made, Celestial Seasonings Tea, which yielded a better than 15 percent annual return over the period she held it.

Meanwhile, she became acquainted with Obie Benz, who had just started the first of the progressive Funding Exchange foundations, the Vanguard Foundation. Tracy joined the thirty other donors and activists in this movement, although leadership from the traditional foundations of the time paid scant attention to this new generation of donors.

It was at this point that Tracy began looking for others like herself in the San Francisco Bay Area: young people with inherited wealth and a social conscience who would be stewards and mentors, who would share, as her mother had, their experiences with fundraising and giving away money. Unfortunately, she could not locate anyone in the local foundation community to work with her. In fact, she found very few peers other than her cousin, George Pillsbury, who came to San Francisco in 1974. Finally, after six years of personally granting $120,000 annually, she found guidance through philanthropy consultant Florette Pomeroy, who helped Tracy and her associates, Marya Grambs and Roma Guy, develop a two-year project to explore the need for a foundation specifically for women. The project led to the creation of the Women's Foundation in San Francisco in 1981, one of the first of its kind in the nation. Since then, Tracy has been part of the national movement to establish women's funds and proudly points to the more than sixty-five currently in existence, many of which she was instrumental in establishing.

When Tracy was active in the Vanguard Foundation, she noted that women consistently deferred to men or became passive when the subject of money arose in a discussion. "I noticed that we all discussed the value of the projects but, even though sixty percent of the group were women, when the subject of money and budget came up, men dominated the conversations." As a result, Tracy and another donor asked sixteen of the women to a retreat by themselves for a day to talk openly and candidly about money. As she explains, "We all said that we were ashamed about how little we knew about money, and so, rather than be embarrassed, we remained silent when the topic came up." Two years later, Tracy was asked to become involved in a San Francisco women's foundation whose mission was to teach women about money management and to raise money for women and girls. "I leapt at the opportunity," she recalls, "because I needed to know more about my money management and knew I could learn from others. We began a series of education programs for about a hundred women and got totally overwhelmed with how much need there was—everyone wanted to come! We scheduled about ten in the first year, with about four or five hundred people signed up for each one and room for only one hundred."

What Tracy and the other organizers learned was that financial education for all women, at all income levels, was of great interest, so they decided to specialize in order to serve all women. For low-income women, the foundation had a grant program. A program called Women's Initiatives in Self-Employment (WISE) targeted middle-income women who wanted to start businesses. The foundation also began a program called Managing Inherited Wealth, which is now a part of Resourceful Women, set up in 1990.

Managing Inherited Wealth

Since 1984, Managing Inherited Wealth has worked with more than two thousand women in the Bay Area with $25,000 or more of inherited wealth. Three hundred to four hundred calls come in to the office annually from women who have heard about the program from others. Tracy reports that the group has not made use of the media or publicized its program because the small staff would not be able to handle any more calls than it currently does. "The response exemplifies the need for more programs like this for women. We do forty financial education programs a year for women and could do hundreds more if we had the money and staff."

Tracy says that she has seen a remarkable change in the women who are involved, due to their self-help programs. She notes that when she first moved to California, most of the middle-aged women she met "did not identify as women donors at all." Many of them had male financial managers or male foundation executives. She vowed not to have that pattern repeated for the next generation and has committed herself to empowering women as philanthropists through financial education programs and support services.

She attributes the success of Managing Inherited Wealth to its being donor-focused and cautions development officers against trying to manipulate women. "It's centered on the woman and what she needs. It's not 'how can we get more money out of this woman so she does our project.' I believe if you are centered on women and come together and ask them what they need, you will grow a healthier program," she explains.

Managing Inherited Wealth is like a twelve-step program, according to Tracy. It consists of a series of sessions with a group of about a dozen women, who work on financial education, share stories, and talk about what Tracy refers to as the psychosocial issues of wealth: money in families, relationships, and work. At the end of every session, Tracy asks the women what topics they would choose if they were to design their own series. Over the past nine years, more than five hundred topics have been proposed, including real estate, loaning money to friends, money and children, and setting up trusts. Financial professionals, therapists, and other specialists are sometimes invited to subsequent sessions.

Tracy has broken the five hundred topics into six major areas, which she calls the "core curriculum":

1. *Identity and self-esteem.* This is the primary issue that women must contend with in assuming control of their finances, according to Tracy. Women need to consider what it means to be a woman in our society, especially a woman who is using her money without exploiting others in the process. Women must also confront the topic of power. Most have a certain amount of resistance to using their power because they have witnessed the abuse of power rather than its positive use, she says.

2. *Basic financial education.* Tracy claims that what women really want is a class in Finance 101. They want to understand the difference between a stock and a bond, for example, along with other fundamental economic theories and definitions.

3. *Choosing and managing financial professionals and financial institutions.* There are a number of nuances at work in this area, according to Tracy, and Resourceful Women has produced a video and a booklet dealing with some of these issues, such as how to hire, evaluate, and communicate with a financial professional.

4. *Getting organized.* Women want practical information on such topics as how to organize their financial information, what they need to do as executor of an estate, and why it is all right to have someone come in and help them with their bookkeeping.

5. *Relationships.* Tracy attributes many divorces, lost friendships,

and family arguments to power battles and secrecy regarding money. Resourceful Women counsels its clients on prenuptial agreements and creative conflict resolution. Periodically, the women's partners and families are invited to join them at a financial discussion session.

6. *Purposeful work and contributions to society.* Both humanity and spirituality underlie all of Tracy's work. Occasionally, Resourceful Women offers a program on money and spirituality to bring a sense of higher purpose to its work and to create a balance between the materiality of money and the intangibility of causes. "We have found, through the program and the empowerment of women, that wealth comes through giving and abundance through giving of ourselves. I really believe that when we extend ourselves, something comes back. Finding that piece of work with your family member, your children, or in the world will give you enormous satisfaction of belonging."

Resourceful Women has sent models of its work to several women's foundations across the country, with the goal of establishing similar programs in twenty-five cities by the year 2000.

The Women Donors Network

Resourceful Women has established a program called the Women Donors Network specifically for women giving $25,000 or more annually to social change charities. It began with a group of women with an astonishing lack of information about their own financial situations. Most said that they did not control or manage the majority of their assets and that many of their assets were tied up in family businesses that they did not understand or know how to get out of.

To spark the women's interest in learning about their personal financial situations, Tracy asked them to imagine that they had complete control over their money and that each could give enough to produce collectively $10 million. What would they do with that money? Purchasing a television network that would give access to women and girls was one idea; the creation of an award program for women was another. (This second suggestion became a reality in 1992 with the launch of the Resourceful Women Awards.) Tracy feels strongly that this "collective" model of raising money greatly appeals to women.

Sixty-five women are now involved with the Women Donors Network, and most give about $100,000 a year, although a few grant from $500,000 to $1 million annually. The average net worth of the women involved in the network amounts to $17 million, and their combined net worth is an estimated $3 billion. Tracy recommends that women in a group or network of this kind anonymously write down their net worth on a piece of paper and then have it tallied up. Resourceful Women also asks its members to submit their donor lists, anonymously if they wish. This gives them a chance to look together at what they give to and why.

Writing a "giving list" is a valuable personal exercise for the women, according to Tracy. She encourages women to get their income tax statements from the past four or five years and review the sheets listing their charities, noting any changes that have taken place. This reveals where their values and interests lie and helps them make decisions based on those values, as opposed to engaging in less well-thought-out "checkbook giving."

Tracy notes that initially many of the women came to the Women Donors Network primarily for basic financial education, and they were not extremely philanthropically inclined. So the network began cultivating their philanthropy. As the women have become aware of their finances and taken control of them, they have also begun planning their philanthropy and giving much more.

Financial Awareness Seminars for Women

Tracy also takes her message on the road in the form of financial awareness seminars for women, sponsored by various nonprofit organizations. These sessions usually open with an appeal for the women to tell their stories. A common thread running through individual women's messages is that they often feel anxious and isolated when it comes to money. To avoid embarrassment and indiscretion, Tracy stresses confidentiality for all involved and asks those attending not to discuss what has been said in the session after they leave. This is done to make the attendees feel it is all right to ask questions and share mistakes made. Also, in a session such as this, women can shed some of their isolation by hearing others' experiences. But most will only do this if the group agrees on complete confidentiality.

To get women talking at a seminar for the University of Wisconsin's Bascom Hill Society Women's Council (see Chapter Eleven), Tracy shared stories of her own experiences learning about money and philanthropy. She described her reluctance to balance her checkbook in timely fashion, her "pockets of chaos" (the piles of paper sitting around waiting to be filed), and some bad financial decisions she had made, including loans to friends. She also talked about some risks that she has taken in her charitable giving, some of which turned out badly. She does not regret having taken the risks, however: "I put the money in the hands of people who had a dream, who believed they could do it. I know they made an investment too and learned something in the process. So did I."

Women Talking About Money

Later in the seminar, Tracy urged the women to take a lead in openly talking about money. For example, she suggested that the women ask their friends questions about money: Do you save money? Do you invest money? How do you do it? And at the year-end gift-giving season, Tracy suggests asking, "What did you give to?" rather than "What did you get?"

The fifty women attending the seminar responded candidly when Tracy asked them to share one example of what they were currently doing in their lives related to money. The replies ranged from preparing or redoing their will to looking at a new business venture. Many of the women also mentioned working with parents or children on their finances. Tracy said that she was investigating how to cut down her own waste of money, simply so that she would have more to give away.

Financial Planning, Risk Taking, and Money Management

Commenting on the number of participants who were working with their families on financial planning, Tracy reported seeing a tremendous sense of responsibility on the part of women to take care of their families and other women and children. "We do have that sense of responsibility for taking care of others, which manifests itself in our own families. Helping our parents or children with their financial planning tends to be women's role as caretakers in families. The responsibility of learning about money and money management is something we know now we cannot postpone. . . . It occurred to me a few years ago that learning about money management was for us like our grandmothers learning to vote . . . and our mothers learning to drive a car. . . . All of these steps represent a sense of opportunity and independence."

Tracy suggested that women commit a certain amount of time each month—four or five hours—to learning about money management. "When I talk with women and ask if they are interested in getting involved, they say, 'absolutely.' Then when I ask if they would like to give, they say they don't have enough money. Further questioning reveals that they don't know how much money they

do have because they can't read the information they get and someone else takes care of their money," she says.

Another primary concern that Tracy discussed frankly was
women's fear that their money will not last; she sees this trait in
women with $10 million in assets just as often as in those who are
$20,000 in debt.

Sharing

Tracy asked three women to come forward and respond to four questions before the group. The women had been contacted earlier and
given the questions in advance so that they could think them over
before the discussion.

1. Describe two of your most important "learning lessons" along
   the way in your money journey.

   Responses depended on the woman's marital status and her relationship within a marriage, ranging from having taken over her husband's business following his death to negotiating the purchase of
   a car.

2. Describe your giving process and who and what inform your
   giving priorities.

   This discussion helped women examine how they were taught
   to give as children and what motivates their giving as adults.

3. How might you improve this process? What additional information or support would you like? What would constitute
   improved gift giving for you?

   The women remarked that just talking about giving makes a
difference, and they liked sharing their stories and learning from
others. Even if they could not give to everything, just learning about

the many different interests represented on the panel was an educational process.

4. Given the state of the world and of your life, how do you feel about the time and money you give now? Think about the percentage of your income or assets that you are committed to giving.

Tracy helped the panel recognize that most people go through various life stages that preclude giving, such as family illness or children's education. Although she did not expect the panelists to announce the percentage of their income or assets they were giving, she feels that it is important to think in those terms.

Evaluating Nonprofits

Tracy recommends a thoughtful approach to philanthropy, as opposed to purely spontaneous giving. She offered specific suggestions for evaluating nonprofit organizations, such as telephoning an organization to request its Form 990, a tax form that shows what is being spent on both administration and fundraising. These forms are required by the Internal Revenue Service on an annual basis. She also advised asking for annual reports, which help show how large organizations, such as the United Way, give away their money.

She pointed out, however, that a fair evaluation of a nonprofit organization's administrative expenses has to take into consideration the age of the organization and what is actually being accomplished by the group. The women's funds, for example, represent a very young movement in the field of philanthropy. In the early phases, a fund can spend 35 cents or even 45 cents out of every dollar on administrative expenses—but that is because it is employing new people, creating advocacy, and changing the face of philanthropy, leading to high administrative expenses while building an endowment. By contrast, established organizations such as the

United Way have had decades in which to build their structure and endowments and can now keep administrative expenses quite low.

Tracy explained that many families are now communicating with each other about the projects they are currently supporting. By copying information for other family members, one can advocate for an organization within the family and obtain even more support.

Small Discussion Groups

For the final exercise in the seminar, the women broke into small groups of five to eight individuals to discuss four more questions concerning giving. This concluding activity was essential, as the women were now ready and even eager to talk openly about money and giving. Following the small group discussions, Tracy led an overall review.

1. What is the most creative thing you have done with your money to date? And your time?

Tracy cautioned the women to note when they were giving without conscious reflection, out of a sense of loyalty, or merely out of habit. She urged them to change the pattern, assuring them that it "will bring more fun and satisfaction into your giving as well. The creativity that you bring to your philanthropy will help sustain your giving."

2. What do you hope to accomplish with your money during your lifetime, and how does this relate to your personal mission?

Tracy asked the women to think about making the connection between financial planning, philanthropic planning, and life planning. She suggested that one way to begin this was to write your own obituary, which will reveal how you want to be remembered.

3. What is a current barrier or problem you face regarding your giving now, and how might you get support to transcend this barrier?

Many women in the Women Donors Network have reported that they would make a pledge to an organization and then wait three to six months to write the check. The network responded by offering a secretarial service for a few hours a week to help the women keep track of their grant making. Grant making can be a very tedious task for wealthy women, as they receive so many solicitations and have to keep track of the requests and the contributions. This is even further compounded by tax consequences, as most report and pay quarterly. If the women have a foundation, lengthy reporting is required.

Another barrier often brought up is that many women do not feel that they own their money, particularly if they obtained it through inheritance or marriage. Tracy recommends helping women develop an entrepreneurial spirit with regard to how they use their wealth:

> But that won't happen until you put women around other women who have invested some or all of their own money, made their own decisions about hiring financial professionals, and shared experiences, such as their husbands giving one million dollars to their universities while they were only giving ten thousand. By becoming engaged in these conversations, women will be encouraged to take some risks, to invest even a small amount of money themselves and see what happens, to notice that others have lost money and they're still OK. This is the entrepreneurial spirit that women can develop by really having a chance to make or lose money through their own decisions. Then they will begin to apply that same entrepreneurial spirit to their giving.

Although some of the University of Wisconsin women cited

current uncertain economic conditions, Tracy reminded them that during the 1980s our asset base increased dramatically in most cases. Then she mentioned the flood that had recently occurred in the Midwest and expressed the hope that some people would consider giving out of their principal because of "the moment of history we're in."

4. What advice about giving and service will you pass on to the next generation?

One woman recalled that she had been given a dime allowance when she was a girl and was expected to put a penny into a box to save for someone who needed it. Another participant reported that she had challenged the other members of her family, including her children, to give to a cause that she wanted to support and that they rose to the challenge. Yet another said that she told her children that she would support their giving by matching their gifts. Tracy proposed that parents encourage their children to give away 10 percent of their allowance. "The children are amazed to see that there is still lots left over after the 10 percent is gone." Tracy also recommended putting a certain amount in a child's bank account each year and then working with the child to give it away. Resourceful Women has recently initiated a program for young people to help them understand money management and giving.

In closing, Tracy asked the women to leave the seminar with a commitment to relax and initiate conversations about money, as Dr. Ruth Westheimer advises people about sex. She admitted that sometimes this is uncomfortable because of differences of equity, race, and class that restrict openness in the subject. "This is integral to discussions about money. Sometimes we hold ourselves back from getting into conversations about money because we don't want to embarrass a person who may not have much. But engage. If the person doesn't have money, maybe there's a way that you can be supportive of that person and in the process provide some education without necessarily becoming obligated in the relationship. I encourage you to ask more questions, and you'll be amazed at how much more abundant your lives will be as a result of the discussion and the answers."

As the women walked off in small groups from the three-hour session, there was a sense of strength not present earlier in the day and a heightened feeling of empowerment. Only through such open and interactive dialogue will we be able to fortify and energize our women donors, and this is a process that we can initiate at our own institutions and organizations. Discussion groups using this format can be led by someone from a community foundation, a woman philanthropist or a respected woman from the financial community. Tracy says, "The results will be amazing as money is demystified and women begin investing in themselves and ultimately move on to investing in your programs."

Asking for Money from Women of Wealth

As a volunteer fundraiser, Tracy has raised millions of dollars. She believes that in working with female prospects, we must look at the ask as an entire process, beginning with the development of the relationship and followed by a candid discussion of the woman's motivations for giving. As a philanthropist, volunteer, and paid fundraiser who still gives 100 percent of her earned income to nonprofits, she shares the following insight about what motivates women's giving: "Women want to know where their money goes and want it to get directly into the hands of people who are in need. My experience is that women don't look at what is going to come back to us personally. We give because we believe. It's a form of letting go. It's saying, 'I believe in you.' The majority of women that I see and deal with do not feel the need, which has been identified as male, to have visible recognition for our gifts. . . . Women care more about people and helping them help other people effectively."

Overcoming Institutional Resistance

Development officers may encounter some resistance as they try to set up separate programs for women within their institutions. Tracy refers to her experiences when she was starting the Women's Foundation in San Francisco. She approached a group of nine men at the *San Francisco Chronicle* and asked them to contribute to the effort.

> They wanted to know why we needed a program or a foundation just to help women. They were all making sports analogies for everything, so I came up with a sports analogy for them. I asked them to imagine that they were soccer coaches and that their daughter and son were on a team. They know that the boys have been playing soccer for many, many years while the girls are just learning the game—they've been doing other types of things, so they are just learning. As coaches, they notice that the girls need more practice kicking the ball, so they pull that group of girls out to strengthen their kicking, just as they periodically pull the boys out to practice certain skills. I pointed out that this was what the Women's Foundation was all about—working with women to strengthen and practice certain skills to help them catch up. It worked. They ended up giving us $50,000 on the basis of this sports analogy. The point is, we're all going to come back and play together at the end.

For more information about Tracy Gary and the Women Donors Network, contact Resourceful Women, 3543 Eighteenth Street, #9, San Francisco, CA 94110; phone (415) 431–5677.

Chapter Thirteen

Conclusion: Realizing the Potential of Women's Philanthropy

Philanthropy is indeed the next frontier for women. And like the American frontier of two centuries ago, it poses both dangers and rewards for those who venture into it. By philanthropy, we mean more than sending a check to a church, public television station, or homeless shelter. We are talking about a planned, deliberate program to improve society. This frontier can be frightening for people who were not brought up in it. There is the danger of squandering one's money on an organization that is not capable of accomplishing its goals because of internal organizational problems. There is also a danger for people who do not understand their own financial situations: not only must they be careful not to jeopardize their own future security, but they also risk some embarrassment if they let on that they are not money-savvy. But these are risks that women can manage with education, courage, and commitment. And the rewards are almost beyond imagination: a sense of financial competence, a role in the decision-making levels of our nonprofit community, a chance to help solve society's problems for the sake of future generations, and, very simply, the joy of giving.

The rewards to nonprofit institutions and society as a whole are equally fantastic. More than just an expanded base of affluent donors, women represent a powerful force for change. Their interests cover a broad range of nonprofit causes, and they give to organizations that are dedicated to social change. Indeed, American women will lead the transformation of the philanthropic community, bringing nonprofit institutions back to their social roots.

In particular, women, with their unique response to fundraising methods, will force development officers to remember why they entered the profession in the first place. It was not for the paycheck, the commission, or the excitement of closing the gift. Indeed, people choose to become fundraisers because they want a chance to help the indigent, to bring art to the public, to save the earth—to make the world a better place. Unfortunately, in a world in which nonprofits compete for limited philanthropic dollars, these core values get lost in the shuffle of the everyday operation of a development office. Women represent an expanded donor base, yes, and they have the potential to bring many more charitable dollars to the table. But they do not respond to the highly technical fundraising approach that has taken over many development operations.

When you consider that women have only recently begun to gain control over their own money, it is not surprising that most have not yet developed expertise in philanthropy. And yet the urge to help and create is there. In fact, data from Case Western Reserve University, UCLA, and the University of Wisconsin, Madison, indicate that women are already giving in greater proportion than they are being asked in our campaigns. It is up to the development profession to raise the philanthropic sights of their women supporters by identifying their needs as donors. Some need fundraisers to teach them how to give. Others simply want permission to follow their hearts.

Fundraisers can make the philanthropic frontier less rocky for women by educating them in financial matters and helping them visualize what they can accomplish with their giving. We can show them how our organizations and institutions can address the social problems they are concerned about. We can also educate them about the financial needs of these organizations—needs that cannot be met with their volunteer efforts alone. We must ask women for gifts in proportion to their representation in our constituency and suggest specific ways to give that will most benefit the program they choose to support and still leave them financially secure.

When women do give, we must thank them (not their husbands) personally and provide recognition that is meaningful. Finally, we must take them seriously as the intelligent, competent, and conscientious citizens they are.

This will call for a transformation in the normal operating procedures of many nonprofit institutions. It is clear that the technical approach to fundraising leaves most women cold. They are generally not moved by a call to compete with their peers by giving a large gift, nor do they care about having their names etched in bronze or marble. The chance to participate in an exclusive golf outing will inspire few women indeed. These are superficial rewards for a very meaningful act. They do not get at the concerns women have for society, which are the real reasons they give.

As fundraisers, we should keep in mind the six C's of women's giving: the desire to change, create, connect, collaborate, commit, and celebrate their philanthropic accomplishments. We must show women how they can *change* the course of society for the better by supporting the work of our institutions. With their philanthropy, they can be entrepreneurs and *create* a program or an opportunity for someone who would not otherwise have any opportunity. By *collaborating* as volunteer fundraisers, they can *connect* with an organization and with other women who share their vision. Their *commitment* to volunteer efforts is well directed when they work to help other women express themselves through giving. And finally, they can *celebrate* their achievements with well-deserved fun.

By establishing programs in our development offices that focus on women's giving, we can reach the women who believe in our institutions' work. We can inspire them not only to give but also to serve as role models. We can train them in how to encourage other women to follow their fine examples. Most of all, we can help them develop an approach to their philanthropy: we can help them develop their voice.

Sylvia Hewlett discusses her own approach to philanthropy in her book *When the Bough Breaks: The Cost of Neglecting Our Chil-*

dren (1991). She points out that saving children is more than "enlightened self-interest." Indeed, she says, we must help children simply because it is the right thing to do (pp. 356–357). Women can express their values while helping future generations by making the world a better place.

Many women now enjoy the improved opportunities that were won by earlier pioneers of the women's movement. They have better jobs, better wages, and more control over their own money than their mothers could ever have dreamed possible. However, these successes and the comforts they can buy do not compare to the satisfaction of giving. These lucky women have the potential to use their hard-won wealth to create a better future—for themselves, their children, and others.

The selfish motives that fueled so many decisions in our nation in the 1980s have resulted in widespread poverty, which has in turn led to increased crime, drug abuse, and tension between factions of our society. While individualism flourished, our basic economic and social unit, the family, foundered. The need to progress from selfishness to altruism is clear: even if we as individuals can hold our families together and see ourselves and our loved ones thrive economically and intellectually, our lives will still be lacking without a healthy society in which to exist.

Through altruism, women can improve the lives of people in need, provide art and culture for everyone in the community, and preserve the natural world we live in. At the same time, by giving, they can discover the true meaning of their existence. Women have made significant gains in many arenas in the past few decades, but it is still only through giving that women (or men) can experience true happiness. By this we do not mean that women should give to family, church, or community to the point of denying their own needs. That kind of giving is not informed, nor does it help express a woman's vision for the future.

As fundraisers, we have a special mission by which we can help women find meaning through informed giving. We can help them examine their values and explore ways to act on their beliefs. Ultimately, women will rise above the need for self-gratification. They will reach the point where, by helping others, they will be rewarded a hundredfold.

This will not be the first time that women will improve society while crossing a frontier in their own liberation. For example, when women won the vote, they forced politicians to begin to address their interests or lose out at the polls. The results of this effort have ranged from child labor laws to required seat belts in automobiles to regulation of polluters. As women realize their potential as philanthropists, they will again improve society while they themselves benefit from the joy that they derive from giving.

Institutions that choose to ignore the great potential of women as philanthropists will be limited not only in financial support but also in the kind of donor commitment that produces true change. Conversely, by changing the focus from closing gifts to building philanthropic partnerships, fundraisers will attract more women as donors. Not only will they profit from the 60 percent of the nation's wealth that women hold, but they will also benefit from the considerable talents and dedication of this neglected half of the population. They will also help women lead the transformation in charitable giving that may well save our society.

References

"About Women and Politics." *Marketing to Women,* Jan. 1993, pp. 1–2.

Abramson, J. "Women's Anger About Hill-Thomas Hearings Has Brought Cash into Female Political Causes." *Wall Street Journal,* Jan. 6, 1992, pp. A1, A14.

Apple, R. W., Jr. "Steady Local Gains by Women Fuel More Runs for High Office." *New York Times,* May 24, 1992, Section 4, pp. 1, 5.

Armstrong, L. "Woman Power at Mazda." *Business Week,* Sept. 21, 1992, p. 84.

"Asian Americans." *Marketing to Women,* Dec. 1991, p. 59.

Bamford, J. "The Working Woman." *Working Woman,* May 1993, pp. 49, 64.

Belsky, G. "The Five Ways Women Are Often Smarter than Men About Money." *Money,* June 1992, pp. 74–82.

Bergan, H. *Where the Money Is.* Alexandria, Va.: Bioguide Press, 1992.

Better, N. "The Secret of Liz Claiborne's Success." *Working Woman,* Apr. 1992, pp. 68, 70–71, 96–97.

"Blacks Who Give Something Back." *Ebony,* Mar. 1990, pp. 64, 66, 68–69.

Boas, L. *Woman's Education Begins.* New York: Arno Press/New York Times, 1971.

Bonavoglia, A. "View from the Top: The Impact of Women CEOs." *Making a Difference: The Impact of Women in Philanthropy.* New York: Women and Foundations/Corporate Philanthrophy, 1991, pp. 1–18.

Brock, P. "Anita Roddick." *People,* May 10, 1993, pp. 101–106.

Carson, E. D. "The Contemporary Charitable Giving and Voluntarism of Black Women." Paper presented at the Center for the Study of Philanthropy, City University of New York, June 1987.

Carson, E. D. *The Hand Up: Black Philanthropy and Self-Help in America*. Washington, DC: Joint Center for Political and Economic Studies, 1993.

Center for the American Woman and Politics. *Gender Gap Fact Sheet*. New Brunswick, N.J.: Center for the American Woman and Politics, Rutgers University, 1992.

Chase, L. *Famous Wisconsin Women*. Madison: Women's Auxiliary of the State Historical Society of Wisconsin, 1971.

Clarke, C. "Karan's Commander-in-Chic." *Working Woman*, June 1992, p. 15.

Collison, M. "More Freshmen Say They Are Choosing Colleges Based on Costs." *Chronicle of Higher Education*, Jan. 22, 1992, pp. A33–36.

"Daughters Already at Work, and Succeeding." *New York Times*, Apr. 28, 1993, p. C1.

Davis, M. W. *Contributions of Black Women to America*. Columbia, S.C.: Kenday Press, 1982.

"Direct Mail Helps Get More Gifts from Apple Computer's Workers." *Chronicle of Philanthropy*, Jan. 26, 1993, p. 30.

Elmer-Dewitt, E. "Anita the Agitator." *Time*, Jan. 25, 1993, pp. 52–54.

Famous Wisconsin Women. Vol. 2. Madison: Women's Auxiliary, State Historical Society of Wisconsin, 1972.

"Finance: Investments Not a 'Man's Job.'" *Marketing to Women*, Apr. 4, 1993, pp. 4–5.

Fisher, J. M. "Celebrating the Heroines of Philanthropy." In A. I. Thompson and A. R. Kaminski, *Women and Philanthropy: A National Agenda*. Madison: Center for Women and Philanthropy, University of Wisconsin, 1993.

Francese, P. "Income Winners." *American Demographics*, Aug. 1992, p. 2.

Freeman, K. C. "For Women, a Time to Close Philanthropy's Gender Gap." *Chronicle of Philanthropy*, June 2, 1992, pp. 40–41.

Friedman, J. "The Founding Mother." *New York Times Magazine*, May 2, 1993, pp. 50, 60, 64–65.

Godfrey, J. *Our Wildest Dreams: Making Money, Having Fun, Doing Good*. New York: HarperCollins, 1993.

Goldman, P., and Mathews, T. "'Manhattan Project,' 1992." *Newsweek*, Nov.–Dec. 1992, pp. 40–42, 55, 56 (election issue).

Goss, K. A. "Young Women Seen as Top Leaders and Backers of Social-Action Causes." *Chronicle of Philanthropy*, Jan. 15, 1991, pp. 21, 24.

Greene, E. "N.Y. Stock Exchange's First Woman Uses Profits to Underwrite Charities." *Chronicle of Philanthropy*, June 16, 1992, pp. 7, 14.

Groer, A. "Women, Power and Politics," *Self*, March 1993, pp. 146–149.

Hall, H. "Women's New Charity Clout." *Chronicle of Philanthropy*, June 16, 1992, pp. 1, 22, 23–25.

Helgesen, S. *The Female Advantage: Women's Ways of Leadership*. New York: Bantam Doubleday Dell, 1990.

Hewlett, S. A. *When the Bough Breaks: The Cost of Neglecting Our Children*. New York: HarperCollins, 1991.

Hodgkinson, V., and Weitzman, M. *Giving and Volunteering in the United States*. Washington, D.C.: Independent Sector, 1992.

Holley, P. "A Mix of Ethics and Investment." *Racine Journal*, Oct. 21, 1992, p. 1E.

Johnson, B. W., and Rosenfeld, J. P. "Factors Affecting Charitable Giving: Inferences from Estate Tax Returns, 1986." *Trusts and Estates*, Aug. 1991, pp. 29–37.

Jones, R. "Big Giver Expects a Liberal Return." *Rocky Mountain News*, Dec. 6, 1992a, p. 27.

Jones, R. "Women Dig Deep to Make Political Voices Heard." *Rocky Mountain News*, Dec. 6, 1992b, p. 8.

"Karla Scherer Channels Anger into Aid for Businesswomen." *The Detroit News*, Feb. 24, 1992, p. 12F.

"Katherine J. Clark, 95, Georgia Preservationist." Obituary. *New York Times*, May 1, 1993, p. 31.

Kimmelman, M. "The Havemeyer Legacy Spotlighted at the Met." *New York Times*, Mar. 26, 1993, pp. B1–B2.

Kotler, P., and Andreasen, A. R. *Strategic Marketing for Nonprofit Organizations*. 4th ed. Englewood Cliffs, N.J.: Prentice-Hall, 1991, p. 283.

Krafft, S. "Window on a Woman's Mind." *American Demographics*, Dec. 1991, pp. 44–50.

Laurence, L. "Taking on Heirs." *Savvy Woman*, June 1990, p. 14.

Lawson, D. *Give to Live*. La Jolla, Calif: Alti Publishing, 1991, p. 283.

Lederer, L. "Funding Strategies for the '90s." *Ms.*, Nov.–Dec. 1991, pp. 38–42 (double issue).

Lerner, G. *The Female Experience*. New York: Oxford University Press, 1992.

"Life After Nannygate." *Working Woman*, June 1993, pp. 49–50.

McCarthy, K. *Noblesse Oblige*. Chicago: University of Chicago Press, 1982.

McCarthy, K. *Women's Culture*. Chicago: University of Chicago Press, 1991.

McDonell, K. M. "Women and Philanthropy." *Philanthropy Matters*, Fall 1992, pp. 8–11.

McDonell, K. M. "African-American Philanthropy Has a Long Rich History." *Philanthropy Matters*, Summer 1993, pp. 2–5.

McHenry, R. *Famous American Women*. New York: Dover Publications, 1980a.

McHenry, R. *Liberty's Women*. Springfield, Mass.: Merriam, 1980b.

Matthews, A. "Alma Maters Court Their Daughters." *New York Times Magazine*, Apr. 7, 1991, pp. 40, 73, 77–78.

Meier, A. *Negro Thought in America*. Ann Arbor: University of Michigan Press, 1963.

Menschel, R. "Women as Contributors to Higher Education." Unpublished report, Cornell University, May 1992.

Millar, B. "Baby Boomers Give Generously to Charities, Survey Finds, but Their Willingness to Do Volunteer Work Is Questioned." *Chronicle of Philanthropy*, July 24, 1990, pp. 1, 13.

Millar, B., "Women's Funds Get 22 percent Rise in Donations." *Chronicle of Philanthropy*, June 15, 1993, p. 16.

"Minorities: Asian." *Marketing to Women*, Dec. 1990, p. 38.

"Minorities/Shopping: Multi-Cultural Shopping Patterns." *Marketing to Women*, Oct. 1992, p. 6.

Morgan, D. Unpublished research, Council for Aid to Education, 1994.

Myers, C. "As Smart as They Look." *Mirabella*, June 1993, pp. 100–111.

Nasar, S. "Women's Progress Stalled? Just Not So." *New York Times*, Oct. 18, 1992, sec. 3, pp. 1, 10.

"New Group Urges Vote by Women." *New York Times*, Oct. 7, 1992, p. A14.

"NFWBO and *Working Woman* Announce 1994 Top 50 Women Business Owners." *NFWBO News*, Summer 1994, pp. 1, 4, 14.

Nichols, J. E. *Changing Demographics: Fund Raising in the 1990s*. Chicago: Bonus Books, 1990a.

Nichols, J. E. "Targeting Today's Working Women as a Rich Source of Potential Gifts." *NonProfit Times*, June 1990b, pp. 1, 96.

O'Hare, L. "Women in Business: Where, What, and Why." *American Demographics*, July 1992, pp. 34–38.

Pearl, D. "Newspapers Strive to Win Back Women." *Wall Street Journal*, May 4, 1992, pp. B1, B8.

Pomice, E. "A Few Good Women and How They're Changing the Way Advertising Addresses Us." *Lear's*, Mar. 1993, pp. 103–107, 130.

Richards, R. "Superfund Set Up to Aid Minority Business." *USA Today*, Aug. 25, 1992, p. 48.

Richman, R., "Special Gifts: Women Put Their Money Where It Really Counts." *Chicago Tribune*, Dec. 13, 1992, Womanews Section, pp. 1, 11.

Rosener, J. B. "Ways Women Lead." *Harvard Business Review*, Nov.–Dec. 1990, pp. 119–125.

Rowland, M. "The Working Woman Investment Outlook." *Working Woman*, Jan. 1992, pp. 57–59.

Scher, L. "Making Money While Making a Difference." *Working Woman*, Feb. 1992, pp. 31–34.

Schmittroth, L. *Statistical Record of Women Worldwide*. Detroit: Gale Research, 1991.

Schneider, S. W. "Jewish Women's Philanthropy." *Lilith*, Winter 1993, pp. 6–12, 29, 38–39.

Seymour, H. *Designs for Fundraising*. 2nd ed. Ambler, Pa.: Fund Raising Institute, 1988.

Shaw, S. C., and Taylor, M. A. "Career Woman: A Changing Environment for Philanthropy." *NSFRE Journal*, Fall 1991, pp. 42–49.

Sublett, D., and Stone, K. *The UCLA Women and Philanthropy Focus Groups, 1992*. Los Angeles: University of California Development Office, 1993.

Tannen, D. *You Just Don't Understand: Women and Men in Conversation*. New York: Morrow, 1990.

Tanner, N. "Single-Sex Education and Fund Raising: Why Have Women's Colleges Been So Successful?" *National Network on Women as Philanthropists Newsletter*, Aug. 1992, pp. 3–4.

Teltsch, K. "New Donors Shake Up Old Ways of Benevolence." *New York Times*, Sept. 15, 1992, pp. B1, B4.

Tiehen, L., and Andreoni, J. "A Charity of One's Own." In A. I. Thompson and A. R. Kaminski, *Women and Philanthropy: A National Agenda*. Madison: Center for Women and Philanthropy, University of Wisconsin, 1993.

Tifft, S. E. "Asking for a Fortune." *Working Woman*, Nov. 1992, pp. 66, 68, 70.

"U.S. Ethnic Diversity to Grow." *Milwaukee Sentinel*, Dec. 4, 1992, p. A3.

Van Til, J. "Adoption Philanthropy: The Wave of the Future?" *NonProfit Times*, Dec. 1992, p. 18.

Waldrop, J. "The Baby Boom Turns 45." *American Demographics*, Jan. 1991, pp. 22–27.

Wamsley, J., and Cooper, A. *Virginia's Women from 1607*. Richmond: Virginia State Chamber of Commerce, 1976.

Winegarten, R. *Texas Women*. Austin, Texas: Eakin Press, 1986.

"Working Women: College Graduates." *Marketing to Women*, Dec. 1991, p. 82.

Wynter, L. "Broker Splits Fees with Her Foundation." *Wall Street Journal*, July 8, 1992, p. B1.

Zinn, L. "This Bud's for You. No, Not You—Her." *Business Week*, Nov. 4, 1991, pp. 86, 90.

Index